MONEY
CONFIDENCE

KERRY HANNON

Post Hill
PRESS

A POST HILL PRESS BOOK
ISBN: 978-1-68261-433-4
ISBN (eBook): 978-1-68261-434-1

Cover Design by Tricia Principe, triciaprincipedesign.com

Caitlin Bonney, Content Development Editor

Portions of the material originally appeared in NextAvenue. org. Reprinted with permission.

not be liable for damages arising herefrom. The fact that an organization or website is referred to in this work as a citation and/or potential source of further information does not mean that the author or the publisher endorse the information the organization or website may provide or recommendations it may make. Further, readers should be aware the Internet websites listed in this work may have changed or disappeared between when this was written and when it is read.

Post Hill Press
New York • Nashville
posthillpress.com

Published in the United States of America

Dedication

To Marcy, who shows me each day the strength and determination it takes to become a money-confident woman.

TABLE OF CONTENTS

ACKNOWLEDGMENTS

I'm grateful to have such a dedicated team of experts to teach me, and women willing to share their stories of how they became money-confident women after the loss of a partner.

I'm passionate about helping women learn to be financially independent and secure. For more than two decades, I have interviewed, studied, and had the opportunity to speak to numerous women from ages 18 to 88, who are making or have wrestled with smart money decisions and taking control of their financial future. I've been inspired by their eagerness to learn and delighted to hear their success stories.

As with any publishing endeavor, there are certain individuals to whom I am particularly indebted for their support and willingness to educate me along the way.

First and foremost, Caitlin Bonney, who served as Content Development Editor, was my guiding light. Caitlin shepherded this project for nearly two years, reporting and fleshing out the critical information provided here. She also tackled many of the technical aspects with determination, grit, and a sense of humor. Caitlin, thanks for pushing and guiding me gently and persuasively.

Other experts who have dedicated their time and expertise to helping me along the way and whose work in this area I admire and deeply appreciate include: Cindy Hounsell, president of WISER, the Women's Institute for a Secure Retirement; Don Blandin, president and CEO of the Investor Protection Trust (IPT) and the Investor Protection Institute (IPI); Diane Harris, former editor in chief of *Money* magazine; Catherine Collinson, president of Transamerica Institute;

Eileen O'Connor, cofounder and managing principal of Hemington Wealth Management; and Lazetta Rainey Braxton, founder and CEO of Financial Fountains.

My deep appreciation to my agent, Linda Konner, of the Linda Konner Literary Agency, whose publishing acumen and trust in my work has driven my mission of emboldening individuals to manage their financial and working lives to build a rich future.

My special heartfelt thanks to Debra Englander, my distinguished editor, for believing in this project and working alongside me for nearly three decades, from our early days together at *Money* magazine to producing my first entrée in the publishing arena, *10-Minute Guide to Retirement for Women*, and onward through a series of books dedicated to improving people's careers and financial lives.

Special thanks to Billie Brownell and Sarah Heneghan at Post Hill Press who were strongly supportive of this effort and patient along the way.

On a professional and personal note, Richard Eisenberg, managing editor of NextAvenue.org, the PBS channel, deserves a special shout-out. Much of the work I've done in recent years involving the field of women and money has been with Rich. He has skillfully guided the way for my column that I write for NextAvenue.org. Portions of that material appear in this book and I urge all my readers to visit the site. Rich, your encouragement and support mean more to me than I can express in words. Onward to more collaborations.

On a personal note, my own *money confidence* is made possible by the support and inspiration of the following board members of Kerry Hannon Inc.:

ACKNOWLEDGMENTS

To the Bonney family—Paul, Pat, Christine, Mike, Caitlin, Shannon, and Piper, too.

To the Hannon family—Mike, Judy, Brendan, Sean, Emily, Jack, Conor, and Brian.

To my brother, Jack, and to my sister-in-law, Charmaine.

To the Hersch crew—Ginny, David, Corey, and Amy; and the Hackels—Stu, Sue, Cassie, and Eric.

To Jonelle Mullen, my friends at TuDane Farm, and Caparino Z.

To my mother, Marguerite Hannon.

And Zena, my road manager.

Finally, to my husband, Cliff, for your love.

INTRODUCTION

The loss of a partner is one of the most traumatic events conceivable. It's shocking in every sense of the word, regardless of whether you've been widowed or divorced. You say, "How can this be happening?" You're ripped apart inside. You're angry and lonely and scared. You're riding an emotional roller coaster, and just when you think it will glide to a resting spot, it takes off like Six Flags' Great Adventure's Kingda Ka at 128 miles per hour, and begins twisting and turning like a corkscrew.

Your world has shifted in a new direction, perhaps without an advance warning, and dealing with complicated money issues is the last thing you want to do. You simply want to shut down, curl up in a ball, and pull the blanket over your head. You desperately need someone else to handle things while you rebuild and make some sense of it all.

But you simply can't. For most women, that's a recipe for financial disaster. To restore your life, you need to get a grip on your finances as quickly as possible. That means figuring out your net worth and your sources of income, devising a budget you can live on comfortably, understanding your tax liabilities, pulling together a winning investing strategy, planning your retirement, and much more.

In the past two decades, I've interviewed and studied hundreds of women ranging in age from their thirties to their eighties, who have found themselves suddenly on their own and woefully unprepared to manage their financial lives. These women have included my own mother, my best friend, and a confident thirty-something work colleague I never suspected would fall to financial pieces when her partner died unexpectedly of an aneurysm, leaving her with two young children. I've walked alongside these women whom I admire and offered advice and a shoulder to lean on, while they navigated their way through the maze of crafting a blueprint for a financially secure future.

What clings to me is that regardless of their situation in life, many women never seriously think about their financial situation until they're no longer riding shotgun. I mean, *really think* about it. It's on the back burner, maybe a yearly checkup with a financial planner, or a snapshot at tax time, but never a laser-sharp, all-hands-on deck, eyes wide open review of their financial picture blended with a partner's.

And the consequences for such a do-nothing attitude can be calamitous. In this book, I've distilled the money guidance I've learned along the way from my research and in-depth interviews with widows, divorcees, and financial planners into a tight guide to help you take control of your finances one solid step at a time and to become a confident woman. This is your road map to get your money life on solid ground.

Who will benefit from this book?

- Women who left money matters to their partners or significant others and now find themselves on their own.
- Women, now alone, who are unsure of their own decisions when it comes to money.
- Women who confidently manage their own money, but are ignorant about how their departed partners managed theirs.
- Women who have never worked outside the home and are now on their own.

- Single women who have been involved in a long-term, live-in relationship that has abruptly ended.
- Women who are married, but suddenly can't rely financially on a partner because he or she has lost a job or has become disabled.

Finding yourself on your own after losing a partner *is* frightening, but you can get through it. You will get to the other side, trust me. The psychological and emotional issues are gut-wrenching, but not life-threatening. The financial impact, though, can be devastating if you don't step out of the shadows and ramp up your money mojo.

Recovering from a loss takes time. Making the effort to learn about money, however, will give you the knowledge and self-reliance to handle your own finances and make the kinds of decisions that will create a secure future. You will survive and thrive.

There's no ideal starting place, but once you begin to put the puzzle together, you will find it gets easier and the pieces begin to naturally fall into place. The key is to be willing to ask questions, to study, and to forge ahead. You may make some mistakes along the way, but go easy on yourself. Give yourself permission to do so. You can't live your life by trying to avoid mistakes. Instead of ducking this life challenge because you're afraid of making a mistake or failing, shift your thinking from "I'm not ready to do that" to "I want to do that—and I'll learn by doing it. It will make a difference in my life."

In the end, you'll discover that financial security is personal freedom. When you're financially fit, you're nimble. You aren't reliant on someone else. You are in the driver's seat. Importantly, when you are not trapped by debt or frozen by financial uncertainty, you have choices, from the kinds of jobs you can accept to where you live and travel. It's liberating.

In the best of all worlds, you would be prepared before things collapse, but I have found that a surprising number of women (and to be honest, many men) aren't. They've grown complacent, or have been too trusting. However, with some planning, a slow, steady approach to investing, and careful budgeting, you'll be able to emerge from your loss with your world in order and your financial feet planted firmly on the ground. This book is designed to help you get to that safe place.

Your goal is to develop a money plan for the short-haul, a working budget for right now, as well as develop an investment strategy for your future needs. Most women will be on their own one day. In fact, the National Center for Women and Retirement Research estimates that, all told, 90 percent of women will be solely responsible for their finances at some point in their lives.

According to the National Center for Health Statistics, women live an average of five years longer than men. Women with partners who are 2.5 years older should expect to be the sole breadwinner of their households for more than a decade, according to a report by TIAA, the leading financial services provider for the not-for-profit market. The expenses of living alone are dramatically higher than when two people can share household expenses, according to Diane Garnick, managing director and chief income strategist at TIAA.

Healthcare and housing expenses in retirement are much higher than most people expect, she says: "They not only represent a large portion of household expenses at retirement, but they continue to dominate budgets as we age. While housing costs can be reduced by downsizing, healthcare costs are not as easy to manage. Unlike housing, healthcare expenses increase with age. This is a major cause of concern as some of the most expensive illnesses tend to occur later in life."

There's more, says TIAA's Garnick. According to the Department of Health and Human Services, from the age of sixty-five forward, men will spend $18,251 on healthcare, whereas women will spend $19,558. This 7 percent additional spending on healthcare can be attributed to women being more likely to have periods where they suffer through a chronic illness and they are much less likely to benefit from a partner-caretaker. They also forecast that healthcare expenses will rise at a rate of 5.8 percent per year between 2015 to 2025, a growth rate that will affect the financial security of many women.

Phew! I know those are a lot of numbers to process, but the fact is women need to be on top of their finances and planning for these future costs.

Let's shift back to right now, though. Consider the following scenarios. If you're a typical woman, being on your own will probably result in a drop in your standard of living. Going from living comfortably on two incomes to trying to squeak by on one is tough, especially if you have children to support.

Furthermore:

- Only a fraction of divorcing women is awarded any form of court-ordered spousal support these days.
- Fewer than half of all women awarded child support ever get the full amount to which they are entitled. The result: The typical woman's standard of living dives in the first year of divorce from a male partner, while the average man's, jumps.
- Roughly 80 percent of widows now living in poverty were not poor before their partners died, according to

the General Accounting Office. In many cases, that's because a large chunk of savings was drained by the partner's medical bills.

- About 40 percent of women and 13 percent of men who are sixty-five and older are widowed, according to the latest Census figures. Also, roughly 9 percent of men sixty-five-plus and 11 percent of women sixty-five-plus were divorced.

Consider this scenario: It was headline news around the globe when Dave Goldberg, forty-seven, Survey Monkey's Chief Executive Officer and the husband of Facebook Chief Operating Officer and *Option B* and *Lean In* author Sheryl Sandberg, died suddenly of heart-related causes while the couple was vacationing in Mexico. She was forty-five at the time. One-third of women who become widows are younger than sixty-five, according to the Women's Institute for a Secure Retirement (WISER). The financial issues they'll immediately confront go far beyond losing an income. Losing a partner in the blink of an eye can be wrenching. Writing about her experience on Facebook, Sandberg called it "completely unexpected hell—the darkest and saddest moments of my life."

Here are some other real-life examples of women who found themselves unexpectedly in the position of dealing with their own finances and their reactions. (To protect their privacy, last names are deleted.)

Melissa and James began dating in high school as first loves. As soon as they graduated from college, they married. While he studied for his doctorate, she supported both of them on her teaching salary. After completing school, James had excellent prospects. Employers from around the country were vying for his talents, and the money was good.

With their two children, ages six and eight, the couple moved from their hometown in Ohio to Connecticut so James could work at a leading pharmaceutical firm. Two years later, Melissa discovered her husband was having an affair with a woman he had met at a scientific conference. When she confronted him, he asked for a divorce.

Melissa was shocked, bitter, and completely unprepared. She and James had been partners for more than twenty years; now, at age forty, she was alone, far from her family, and had two small children to raise on a modest teaching salary. James claimed he had no assets and was saddled with huge credit card debts. "He was finally starting to make some money, and I was planning to take some time off to spend with the kids," says Melissa. "Now I've got to fight him just to get child support."

Susan's husband, Craig, died of kidney cancer. At age thirty-six, she was left to raise their children, ages three and five. She had no job and no credit in her own name. Although her husband had been sick for three years, she was so wrapped up in caring for him that she never thought about how she'd manage without him. All of a sudden, she had $115,000 in life insurance money and didn't know what to do with it. Wisely, she put her money in a money market account and signed up for a financial planning course at a community college. "I'm not sitting pretty, but I'm on my way to meeting my financial goals," says Susan.

Claire divorced her first husband after thirteen years, when their children were ages six and three. At the time, she was the breadwinner, bringing in $120,000 from her landscaping business. Her ex, who was unemployed, got the house in the divorce proceedings. Then her business went bust, and she was left with nothing.

She started another business painting T-shirts and crafting jewelry as a way to scrape by. Four years later, she remarried, to a successful investment banker who encouraged her to quit work. A few months later, he died of a heart attack without a current will. She quickly returned to work to keep the household solvent, but it was a struggle she will never forget. "Even with my business background, I hadn't taken the time to find out where any of the financial papers were kept," says Claire. In the end, she was unable to recover thousands of dollars invested with out-of-state brokerages.

Rebecca and Ellen had lived together for eight years, but had only been married for one year when Ellen, then thirty-eight, was diagnosed with ovarian cancer. "We kept most of our accounts separate for years, and it was only after we were legally married and started thinking about adopting a baby that we began to combine some accounts," says Rebecca. "We had waited to purchase a home until we were married as well, so when Ellen died two years later, many of our accounts were still scattered," she says.

"Plus, I didn't even know where she had all her passwords stored for her credit cards and investment accounts. We *were* working with a financial planner and did have an attorney who helped us do our wills when we were married, so that helped a lot. But we were so caught up in her medical care and believing she would beat it that we never made a plan for what would happen to her estate if she didn't."

When Laurie, in her mid-fifties, screwed up the courage to file for divorce from her husband of nearly three decades, she had a rude awakening. By all accounts, he was living the high-life with a multimillion-dollar home in one of the country's richest waterfront enclaves. He kept a residence in that state for financial reasons he said. There with no personal income tax levied there, and it was one where he could troll for wealthy new clients.

He chartered private jets to visit his daughter and Laurie and to wing his way to vacation spots to ski or bask in the sun, while regularly bragging about his well-heeled clientele who invested their money with him. But when her lawyer demanded disclosure of assets, he claimed to be broke and dying, beset by many maladies. She had some income from sporadic sales of her artwork, but had relied on his monthly checks deposited to her checking account to cover expenses for her daughter and herself. Once she filed for divorce, he claimed they had been separated for years, valuing his existing estate, which she had to hire forensic accountants to uncover, at far less than it would be at the time she decided to call it quits and take back her own life.

Chances are you will relate to some aspects of these women's stories. For each one, the transition to life alone was swift and painful, but each woman succeeded though tenacity and hard work. None of them found the change to be an easy one, but they're moving forward with their lives.

For every newly single woman, there's a different set of circumstances to navigate. It's messy. No one else is going to have the same situation.

The reality is that a few items must be dealt with immediately. Your decision to read this book is your first step to rebuilding your financial life.

In full disclosure, I've been married for twenty-five years to Cliff, but I still struggle to talk to him about our finances. Fortunately, I do know where he keeps his passwords and stores his important documents. He knows where mine are as well. We have wills. But the truth is, we don't have children, and though we do have joint investment and bank accounts and own our home jointly, we have separate investments and retirement accounts as well. We also own physical assets separately, such as our cars.

That said, our lifestyle is dependent on our shared resources both from income and investments. He's my ballast. The hitch is Cliff is nearly seven years older than I, so even if we do remain happily married for another quarter century, I'm well aware I will be managing solo one day, so I try to stay abreast of our total financial scenario, and we meet regularly with our financial planner.

So, as you begin your journey to single sanity and build your financial acumen, know that you are not alone, and one day, you may find yourself reaching out and paying it forward by helping another woman navigate this path with strength and grace.

Money-confident women, let's go.

CHAPTER ONE

GETTING IT TOGETHER

Knowing where the important financial documents are located can be a stumbling block. It's not unusual for some of these things to fly below your radar before a crisis happens. You might not have a grip on what insurance policies you and your partner have, or know every brokerage account, or other investments you two have amassed over the years.

That certainly complicates this life passage, but I will help you sort through it all. In a divorce, for example, not having transparency about accounts might allow your ex to waltz away with assets you never even knew were rightfully yours, or to hide them in accounts you don't even know exist. And if your partner has died, it can leave you without access to cash from life insurance policies, retirement plans, pension plans, and other benefits for months or longer, depending on how much time it takes you to find the documents. You might even have to hire a forensic accountant to do the sleuthing for you, as the divorcing Lauren had to do when her husband pleaded poverty.

If you're fortunate, your partner and you keep all your important papers in an orderly fashion in a safe-deposit box or a fireproof home safe. In today's digital world, you might even have an external hard drive, or a USB flash drive as an extra level of protection backing up all those documents.

There are also a growing number of encrypted, web-based, and cloud-based storage services to back up and store your important papers. One layer of protection, for example, is FidSafe (fidsafe.com), a secure, online safe-deposit box, to save digital backups of electronically scanned essential documents such as bank and investment account statements, birth certificates, insurance policies, passwords, tax records, wills, and more. Monthly fees range from $7.49 for up to five financial accounts to $22.99 for unlimited accounts and monthly credit reports. Moving forward, I highly recommend you take these kinds of precautions.

But most of us are simply not financially organized to cope with a death or divorce overtaking our lives. We give lip service to our desire to neatly track our financial life, but frequently it's more talk than action. We toss monthly bills in one file, brokerage statements in another, and pension updates in yet another. Some documents we may keep in our home offices, others in bank safe-deposit boxes. Your attorney may hold copies of your wills in his or her office, for instance. You may have absolutely no idea where some items are—say, your marriage certificate or partner's birth certificate.

In the weeks following your partner's death or during and following divorce proceedings, you will be forced to make dozens of decisions about both your personal and your financial life. So it's critical to know what you have to work with. For widowed women, this can be an especially difficult interval if your partner was sick for a period of time, causing you to focus on doctors, hospitals, and his or her fight for life rather than on money issues. Everything but the life-and-death struggle was likely put on hold.

Getting your finances in order straightaway might seem like a dreaded task, but it will make life easier soon enough.

Women who are separated but not yet divorced should pull this material together as quickly as possible, before the divorce proceedings. It is vital documentation for your attorney to have in order for you to get the best settlement possible.

Believe it or not, while everything else in your life seems to be out of control, this is one area you *can* control. You just have to get organized. And that means locating all the important financial documents.

To find out what assets you have to work with, you might need to do some detective work, but push yourself to get going. Managing money involves knowing what you have—everything from your bank accounts to brokerage accounts to retirement plans—and keeping an orderly system of paperwork.

HERE ARE THE PAPERS YOU WILL NEED TO LOCATE

- ☐ Copies of your joint tax returns for the past five years
- ☐ Records of both your partner's and your retirement accounts
- ☐ All insurance policies, including homeowner's, auto, health, life, and disability
- ☐ Current statements for all bank and brokerage accounts
- ☐ Current statements of mutual fund holdings
- ☐ The deed to your home or your domicile lease agreement
- ☐ Any business partnership agreements
- ☐ Birth certificates
- ☐ Marriage certificate

- ☐ List of credit cards and the names under
  which they are listed
- ☐ Title to your vehicle, car loan information,
  or lease agreements
- ☐ Most recent mortgage statement
- ☐ Employer stock-option plans
- ☐ Wills, living wills
- ☐ Powers of attorney
- ☐ Receipts for major purchases
- ☐ Warranties
- ☐ Prenuptial or postnuptial agreements
- ☐ User name and passwords for online
  banking, investment accounts, social media

WHERE IS YOUR MONEY COMING FROM?

Now that you have all your documents assembled in one place, you can begin to get a feel for your financial picture. You may not understand exactly what it all means, but just gathering the paperwork will take you a long way toward getting it all together. In essence, these documents represent a snapshot of your total assets and liabilities. And that is what you are going to have to work with in the days and weeks ahead.

These are your tools, so to speak. In later chapters, I will discuss how you will use this information to move forward. For example, you'll need this material to establish a budget, figure out your net worth, and develop a financial plan. This is the only way you can accurately determine your financial situation.

You might have trouble locating some of these vital papers. Relax. What you need to do is think about who might have a record on hand. For example, your partner's insurance agent is sure to have a copy of his or her policy in the files. Employers will have records of pension plans, an attorney will have the will, and so on.

The following list represents the kinds of assets you can expect to find outlined in those important papers. Of course, not all of these sources of money will be available to you.

RETIREMENT ASSETS

Annuity: This is a type of investment in which you or your partner, as policyholders, make payments to an insurance company. The money grows tax-free until you withdraw it at retirement. It earns interest and assures you a steady income as long as you live, or for a set time frame.

Defined benefit plan: This is a traditional pension plan in which an employer uses a formula based on salary and years of employment with the firm to devise an income to be paid to the employee or beneficiary on a regular basis at retirement.

401(k) plan: A retirement plan in which the employee makes regular, tax-deferred contributions from a salary each pay period. Often, the employer matches a percentage of the contribution. The employee then selects from a menu of investment choices into which the funds are divided. Vesting is the employee's right to receive the employer-contributed funds after a set number of years of employment.

403(b) plan: Similar to a 401(k), these plans are offered to public employees and people who work for nonprofit organizations.

Traditional Individual Retirement Account (IRA): A tax-deferred pension plan that currently allows many people to invest up to $5,500 annually if under age fifty and $6,500 if fifty and older. Contributions are typically tax-deductible. The account is tax-free until you withdraw the money at retirement. Usually there is a penalty for removing the funds before age 59½, and you must start withdrawing the money at age 70½.

Roth IRA: Unlike traditional IRAs, the contribution is not tax-deductible, but withdrawals are tax-free. Any earnings, however, on the amount withdrawn before age 59½ are taxable. The contribution amount is subject to income limits.

SEP-IRA (Simplified Employee Pension): A retirement plan for someone who is self- employed. There are limits, but contributions are tax-deferred until retirement. Two alternatives are the Solo 401(k), and the SIMPLE IRA.

Social Security: These are retirement funds paid by the federal government, provided the person has been employed for at least forty quarters.

Veterans benefits: These are funds paid by the federal government through the Veterans Administration to individuals who served in the U.S. military.

Health Savings Account (HSA): These accounts must be paired with an eligible high-deductible health insurance plan. The money you put into the accounts is tax-free. It grows tax-free and is tax-free when used for health-related qualified medical expenses for you, your partner, or a qualified dependent. Your HSA balance rolls over from year to year, so the earlier you start, the better, because you can give your money more time to grow tax-free. HSAs can be invested in mutual funds, stocks, and other investments.

INSURANCE POLICIES

Cash value life insurance: Policies such as whole life, variable life, and universal life that are a combination life insurance policy and investment savings plan.

Term life insurance: For a specified period, an annual premium provides a death benefit to survivors.

INVESTMENTS

Bonds: This is a debt of a corporation or the government. A bond buyer provides money to the institution, and it in turns pays back the sum with interest at a specified time.

Mutual funds: A selection of stocks and bonds or a mixture of investments that are pooled together, sold as shares to individual investors, and managed by a professional money manager. Or, is an index mutual fund or exchange-traded fund (ETF) that tracks a specified basket of underlying investments like the S&P 500 or the Dow Jones Industrial Average.

Stocks: These are shares in a company that are sold to raise capital. There are approximately 5,700 publicly traded companies in the United States.

BANK ACCOUNTS

Certificate of deposit (CD): An insured bank deposit with a guaranteed interest rate that is held for a set time period, usually three months, six months, one year, or five years.

Checking: A federally insured bank deposit that typically pays a low interest rate, but does not require any set time period before the funds are available. Payments to others are direct via paper checks or electronic means.

Money market: A federally insured bank account that typically pays higher interest than a regular savings account and requires a minimum investment.

Savings: A federally insured bank account that pays a higher rate of interest than a checking account and is liquid, but there are no check-writing capabilities.

OTHER ASSETS

Proceeds from real estate sales: The net amount received from the sale of a home, vacation house, or other property.

Proceeds from the sale of a business: The amount of money you may receive should a privately held business ownership be sold.

MAKE ROOM TO WORK

The next step is to set up an area in your home that you can use to work on the materials at hand. Some women just lay it all out on the dining room table and sort through the various files as needed. This will take time, so be prepared to forego the use of that piece of furniture for months or even a year or more. Others use one room of the house as a base of financial operations. Everything is stored there, and copies of all correspondence are kept on file.

Next, try to schedule a certain chunk of time each day to devote to the task at hand, and *stick to it*. Accomplishing even one task per day will give you some semblance of order and get the process under way. Action is empowering, even if it only entails making a single phone call or sending one letter.

Once you've assembled all the papers and developed a filing system that makes it easy to find information on an as-needed basis, it's time to take stock of advisors and friends who might help you make sense of it all. This is your board of directors.

WHO CAN YOU TURN TO FOR FINANCIAL GUIDANCE?

Even if you've been blindsided by recent events, my guess is you know more than you think you do about managing your money. While our mothers or grandmothers might have relied on their partners' salaries, that is less the case today with some 72 million women now working. This means we need to know about our money in order to make choices about our employer retirement plans and trim our income taxes, among other things, so chances are you have some working basic building blocks in place.

Moreover, it's no longer considered unfeminine to be knowledgeable about money and investing. Then, too, as we marry later in life, many of us long ago abandoned the outdated notion that we would marry someone who would take care of us for the rest of our lives and we'd never have to worry our pretty little heads about money. We began to accept responsibility for our money lives and started saving and investing in our twenties rather than waiting for a partner to do it for us as many of our mothers did.

It's quite possible you have even been the primary money manager, or CEO, of your household, handling the finances. Or maybe you and your partner shared the duties and worked in tandem to make investment decisions.

That financial knowledge will certainly serve you well in the future. But if you're like most women, financially capable or not, when your partner has died unexpectedly or your marriage has collapsed, you're going to have a hard time focusing on your money matters without some professional guidance to steer you through your emotions with an eye to business. This is, after all, You Inc. You are running your own business and these financial assets are its lifeblood.

For Marty, age forty-three, whose husband died in a car accident, one of the most difficult adjustments was learning to make financial decisions on her own. "We always made the big decisions together," she says. "I wrote the checks, but he dealt with the insurance agent, our financial advisor, and our accountant. I had never even done our income taxes before. That blew me away," she recalls.

Now is the time to make a list of the professionals you might need to contact for advice and help in sorting out your sources of income and putting together an investment strategy. You'll want to include their street and email addresses as well as phone and fax numbers. To start assembling your future advisors, you should ask yourself who has helped you and your partner deal with your money matters in the past.

- Do you have a stockbroker you use regularly? Do you trust this person and feel comfortable continuing to invest with him or her, or will you need to find a new one?
- Do you have a financial planner? Is there a trusted family member or friend who can conncct you with professionals with whom they currently consult?
- Do you have an accountant and an attorney who will have *your* interests as a priority? This is critical for divorcées who may have shared these professionals with their partner.
- Is there a personal banker or a trust officer who handles your accounts?
- What about an insurance agent?
- Who can give you the information you need about your partner's employee pension plan?

One caveat: You may need to hire some new professionals to work with you as you make your transition, particularly in the case of a divorce, where you and your partner both worked with the same individual. I will share resources on how to do so in upcoming chapters.

YOUR MONEY MAKEUP

While you are in the questioning mode, take some time for some soul-searching and to sketch out your overall attitude about money. Before you start to actively manage your assets you should have some inner understanding about how you relate to money, as well as your individual scenario at the present time and what it could be in the future. We all have a different money profile and it will reflect on the choices we make.

Grab a notebook or open a Word document on your laptop and write or type out your responses to the following questions. Take your time. This is not a test. This exercise, though, will help you get a better feel for your financial profile and will come in handy when you start making critical decisions about your money in the days and months to come.

- What's your age?
- What is your biggest fear about money?
- What worries you most about your current money situation?
- Are you currently employed? If so, is your job secure?
- Do you need to find a job? What are the possibilities? What are your skills? Would you need to go back to school or add skills to pivot back to the job market?
- What's your current individual income?
- What are your financial goals? Do you want to be able to travel, keep your home, buy a new car?
- Do you have any health conditions that are a recurring expense for medication or therapy?
- Are you a saver or a spender?
- Are you a conservative or an aggressive investor? One way to look at this is to ask yourself: If the speed limit on the highway says 55, how fast do you usually go? Be honest. There are no cops clocking you.
- If you had $1,000 to invest, would you put it in a guaranteed investment like a money market account or a CD (certificate of deposit), or would you invest it in

a noninsured mutual fund that will rise and fall with the market?

- How important is it to you to spend money on material goods like clothes or vacations?
- How important is it to spend on philanthropy?
- What kind of lifestyle have you been living? Will you have to scale back? How difficult will that be for you?
- Will you inherit money one day? How much is it likely to be and how soon?
- Do you see yourself as a financially independent person or a dependent one?
- Are you a knowledgeable investor?
- Do you tend to take other peoples' advice about investing, or are you a do-it-yourselfer capable of conducting your own research?
- Do you know how to budget?
- What money role did you play in your relationship? Were you the bill payer, the investor, the budgeteer?
- What role did your partner play in your financial life?
- Do you have children to raise and educate?
- Can you support yourself and your children on your own income or financial resources?
- Are you an indulgent parent?
- Will you be able to spend less on your children and not feel guilty?
- Will you have to support your parents one day, or do you already?
- If you are working, how many years until you plan to retire?

While these questions cover a sweeping money landscape, your answers will let you begin to draw a portrait of yourself in relation to money. You'll definitely find this knowledge helpful as you begin to build your own financial life. It will align your inner compass when it comes to making money decisions for today and in years to come.

In the next chapter, widows will learn which tasks must be handled immediately and which phone calls and decisions can be postponed for a while.

It's important to learn this distinction because there are only so many hours in a day. Just because you're on your own now doesn't mean the rest of the world has come to a screeching halt. You may very well be working a full-time job, running a household, and juggling countless other day-to-day activities that make demands on your time. Few of us can dedicate entire days to straightening out the paperwork and getting up to speed financially. No doubt "first things first" will take on a whole new meaning to you.

CHAPTER RECAP

In this chapter, we discussed how to:

☐ Gather your essential money documents
☐ Map out your sources of income
☐ Find who to turn to for financial guidance right now
☐ Discover your money persona

CHAPTER TWO

ACTIONS FOR WIDOWS

It's tough—both emotionally and financially—to be prepared when your partner dies. Even people who are the most forthright about money, financial planning, and investing dance around the discussion of death. The simple task of writing a will is problematic for many people.

There never seems to be the right time. Even a discussion about buying life insurance is somehow seen as morbid. It's not unusual for couples who have been together for years not to have an updated will or the appropriate life insurance coverage.

The shock and emotional and psychological jolt of a death is shattering, though, and without some of these basic protections in place, your world can turn truly chaotic in a blink of an eye. Hopefully, you and your partner have taken the time to talk about what would happen when one of you dies. Perhaps you've even taken steps to prepare. You'll be in far better shape if you have. Too often, the most intense education of your life begins at a time when you are in a state of emotional distress and least able to process it and make clear decisions.

It's normal to feel numb and out of control. But there are several things that you simply must handle—soon. And truthfully, only you can make this happen. Some things are fine to put on hold until you have survived the initial wave and begun to adjust to your new lifestyle. Things are busy at first, with lots of people checking in on you and offering to lend a hand, but that ends and things can get very quiet. People move on and back to their own lives. And that will be the time when you can focus, and really dig into action and formulate your financial plan.

For now, here are your first moves.

Find a grief counselor, therapist, or support group. No one can afford emotionally to be alone at this time. Your church, temple, or another group may be able to make recommendations for you. You'll never be able to tackle your finances until you have some kind of psychological and emotional support system in place. Once you have that to lean on, you can move into the actual tasks at hand.

Joyce McCue and her husband of thirty years, Richard, moved to McLean, Virginia, from Memphis for his job as vice president for Hilton International. Six months later, he learned he had throat cancer. He died a year after their transfer at the age of fifty-five.

Her spouse had a $2.5 million life insurance policy. But when it came to what to do with it and other family investments, McCue was at a loss. "I was always totally bored when we went to our financial planner," she told me. "I controlled the day-to-day finances. I paid the bills. I balanced the checkbooks. But (Richard) did the big-picture stuff."

She did have one thing in her favor: She knew how to control her spending. "Richard and I always teased each other," she said, "because my motto was always, 'Do we need that?' and his motto was, 'Let's get two.'"

She hired a financial advisor, Eileen O'Connor, co-founder of Hemington Wealth Management in McLean. "It was quite intimidating," Joyce recalled. "I felt like I was asking questions a kid in high school would."

And she joined a women's support group. "Widows are able to share and help each other with the challenges they're facing and resources," O'Connor explained to me. "While I'd like to think I'm helpful to my widowed clients, I think they find as much support, or more, from peers that are going through the same ordeal."

Don't make any huge financial decisions soon after your partner's death. Most financial planners, like O'Connor, suggest that widows refrain from investing or spending any lump sum insurance or pension payout at least for six months and ideally, a year. "We always recommend that widows avoid making any big decisions in that first year," says Suzanne Schmitt, vice president for family engagement at Fidelity Investments. That typically means sitting tight with your current investments and refraining from investing any lump sum insurance or pension payout. "Don't make any irrevocable decisions with lump-sum proceeds until you have had the time to fully review your finances and develop a thoughtful financial plan," she adds.

Be careful about overspending early after the death of a partner. One woman I know used her partner's life insurance policy to buy her daughter a car. She meant well and it temporarily made her feel better, but it was money she really needed to sock away for her own future.

Until some time has passed and the fog has lifted, the best place to stash the money from any large insurance policy, for example, is in a money-market fund or money-market account, short-term certificates of deposit, or Treasury bills. While these accounts are probably too conservative for the long term, they provide a good place to invest your money for the immediate future.

That said, you're going to feel pressure from friends, family, and financial advisors to make decisions. The unsolicited advice is probably very well-intentioned, but you'll be better off if you stick to your own schedule.

In the weeks after your partner's death, you're going to be swamped with paperwork. You shouldn't feel that everything is falling on your head and that you need to decide everything now. In fact, the worst thing you can do is make important decisions in haste because you're feeling stressed.

Focus on pressing financial decisions. These include collecting death benefits and ensuring cash flow. "My advice to a recent widow is that we first deal with only the essentials," says Cheryl J. Sherrard, a Certified Financial Planner and director of Financial Planning at Clearview Wealth Management in Charlotte, North Carolina. "There will be a lot of moving parts right after a death and although there are a few items which must be dealt with immediately, the rest can be tabled for a time to give the widows time to get organized and able to emotionally handle the next steps."

Find your important documents. One stumbling block for many widows is knowing where the money is. As I discussed in the last chapter, that often requires some sleuthing to locate savings accounts, brokerage accounts and retirement plans— and identifying the proper online passwords. "The first step to piecing things together," says Eleanor Blayney, author of *Women's Worth: Finding Your Financial Confidence* and consumer advocate of the Certified Financial Planner Board of Standards, "is digging out your joint tax returns for the past five years."

"An ounce of prevention is everything," Blayney adds. "Anticipating widowhood is tough, but the more financial information a woman can gather in advance of the loss of a spouse, the smoother it will be."

Same sex couples review your benefits. If you're in a same-sex marriage, you are entitled to all of the same state and federal benefits as opposite-sex married couples. This means federal benefits, such as Social Security death benefits and COBRA continuation insurance coverage, will apply.

These rules do not apply, though, to unmarried couples who have established either a domestic partnership or civil union. If you're in either of these scenarios, none of the benefits of marriage under federal law will apply to you, because the federal government does not recognize these same-sex relationships. For example, you may not file joint federal income tax returns with your partner, even if your state allows you to file your state tax returns jointly. I recommend that if you want learn more about the rights and benefits available to same-sex couples, consult a lawyer who specializes in this area in your state.

Take daily action. Try to schedule a certain chunk of time each day to devote to urgent financial tasks, and stick to it. I will get to your specific steps shortly. Accomplishing one task a day will give you a semblance of order and can be empowering.

"Many widows get in too much of a hurry to make everything alright, to get back to a 'normal' that feels better," says Sherrard. "What they need to realize is that they are not going to feel normal again for a considerable period of time. Grief takes time."

Be wary. Watch out for unscrupulous people trying to get you to invest with them, too. "Understand there will be those who

prey on the widow," says Sherrard. "There are the complete
strangers who scan the obituaries looking for new business."

Indeed, widows need to make their initial financial moves
cautiously. "There's a sense of urgency to do something right
after you lose a spouse, but I caution widows to recognize the
psychological trauma and don't do anything hastily," says
Blayney. "Widows, in particular, have to be very careful about
being taken advantage of by people who may or may not have
their best interests at heart."

Even well-intentioned relatives may offer advice that
works for them, but which may be off base for you. Pass on it
for now. Wait until your head has cleared.

Work with a financial advisor. This might, however, be an
especially opportune time to find and work with a financial
advisor, especially if your partner had been responsible for
paying the bills and managing the investments (even Sheryl
Sandberg said her husband was the one handling the family's
finances). That's why one of your first moves after the funeral
should be to connect with a Certified Financial Planner. "Some
women are heads of households and managing it all," according
to Danielle Howard, a Certified Financial Planner at Wealth
by Design in Basalt, Colorado, "but probably 75 percent of
women I've worked with just go, 'I am not good at math.' It is
not a matter of being good with math, I tell them. You can use
a calculator. You just need to be comfortable talking about it."

For unbiased guidance, look for a fee-only planner with
the Certified Financial Planner (cfp.net) designation. Ask for
recommendations from friends or from your CPA or lawyer.
You may also want to search for a planner who lives near you
and specializes in working with women and widows; you can
do a search on the websites of the National Association of

Personal Financial Advisors (napfa.org), the Financial Planning Association (onefpa.org), and the Garrett Planning Network (garrettplanningnetwork.com). Another excellent source of financial advice is the Association for Financial Counseling and Education (AFCPE.org) website. An Accredited Financial Counselor (AFC) can address your immediate money challenge and help you create a plan to achieve your goals. You can search by location and area of expertise. Fees for fee-only financial advisors typically start around $200 an hour, but they do vary. Virtual sessions are possible.

Ramp up your education. You may also want to use this time to ramp up your understanding of the basics of personal finance. Howard urges her clients to increase their financial literacy. "That education is vital to getting your feet back on the ground," she says.

One excellent book I recommend is Jonathan Clements' *How to Think About Money.* "We want to seize control of our finances, so we have more control over our lives," he writes. I wholeheartedly agree. The goal, he notes, isn't to get rich. "The goal is to have enough money to lead the life we want."

Online, visit the Investor Protection Institute's site at www.iinvest.org, which offers free guides that explain stocks, bonds, and mutual funds. Three other fine money sites oriented toward women are: DailyWorth.com, LearnVest.com, and WISERwomen.org.

Put your loss in perspective as motivation. One-third of the women who become widows are younger than sixty-five, according to data from the Women's Institute for a Secure Retirement, known as WISER (wiserwomen.org), a nonprofit organization dedicated to women's financial education and advocacy. The Census Bureau reported in 2011 that the median age of widowhood was 59.4 for a first marriage and 60.3 for a second marriage. For many women, the road to financial hardship begins after their partners die. Nearly one-third of single women over age 75 are living in poverty, according to WISER's research.

Like most widows, you will probably be living on a lot less than before your partner died. "The big-picture look at widows is that there's almost always a loss of income," says Cindy Hounsell, the founder and president of WISER. For women in an opposite-sex marriage, take note: women generally live longer than men, making it even more important that they plan their finances carefully.

Consider where to live. An important decision can be where to live. "That's an emotional one because the family home is often the locus of the marriage," Blayney says. "It's not just a financial decision; it is a very emotional decision."

Pump the brakes for now, though. You probably shouldn't move from your home immediately, but as time goes by you might want to consider it to cut costs. Initially, hanging onto your home can be comforting. But eventually the upkeep can dig into any kind of fixed-income principal you're depending on, and the taxes and other home-related expenses, such as lawn care, can really bust your budget.

There's no rush to switch utility and telephone accounts to your name if they are in your partner's name. Keeping a phone in your partner's name, for a time can ward off those unwanted salespeople who prey on widows. Credit card companies should be notified, but this can wait until you have established credit in your own name by getting your own credit card, if you haven't already done so. Eventually, you will want to notify all clubs, alumni groups, and other organizations to which you and your partner belong. Some clubs may let you retain a membership at reduced dues.

ROUND ONE: YOUR ACTION STEPS

Obtain death certificates. You'll need to make about two dozen copies of your partner's death certificate. You'll be required to send this document to everyone from credit card companies to the mortgage holder and his or her insurers to verify the death. It's best to make all these copies at once, then stick them in a file to send as needed.

Notify the deceased's employer. Notify your partner's employer and file for any benefits owed to you, such as pension income, life insurance payouts, and health insurance coverage. To do so, contact the person in charge of employee benefits; usually the human resource department can direct you. Your letter should state clearly your partner's full name and Social Security number, the date he or she died, and a request for information on widow's benefits.

Ask if there are any settlement options for you to consider. If your partner had pension benefits, you may have a choice between lump sum or lifetime payments. Be sure to provide a phone number where you can be reached if there are any questions.

You may need to contact more than one employer if your partner qualified for more than one plan. Administrators for other retirement plans, such as IRAs or Keoghs, should be notified as well. If you were named beneficiary (that is, the person designated to receive the proceeds), these assets can be invested in your own tax-deferred account.

Change beneficiaries. You should also change the beneficiary on any of your own retirement accounts if your partner had previously been named.

Pay your bills. It's easy to stuff them in an envelope for later, but you'll regret it. In addition, be sharp-eyed and don't pay any bill that looks unfamiliar. You might consider setting the recurring ones up on auto-pay. It's unfortunate but this is a time when all sorts of unscrupulous types surface in hopes of getting some free money. Scrutinize every bill carefully to be sure it is legitimate. Be sharp-eyed, and don't pay any bill that looks unfamiliar. Ask for verification from the creditor if the bill doesn't look right to you.

Anne's husband, for instance, bought a Ferrari with cash three weeks before he committed suicide. About six months after the funeral, the dealer who sold him the car contacted Anne and told her that the car had never been paid for and he was going to have to repossess it if she didn't pay up. Fortunately, after some frantic searching, she found a receipt, and the dealer quit hassling her.

Creditors aren't so softhearted these days that they will give you a bereavement grace period. Failure to make your monthly payments can result in onerous interest charges, late fees, and a tarnished credit record that can haunt you for years.

So clear off a work space, pull out a clean financial ledger, and divide your bills, your partner's bills, and your joint debts. Then note the debtor, the total amount owed, and the minimum payment required. (Of course, if the funds are available, it's always best not to carry recurring debt, so paying credit card bills in full is best if you can swing it.) You'll need to pay as many of these as you can in a timely fashion. You'll want to pay your bills and the joint bills, if possible. Your partner's bills should be handled by their estate.

Get a snapshot of your spending. This will help you prioritize expenses while you get a sense of your income, notes financial planner Howard. Make a list of all your debts in the next 30 days and create a manageable spending plan.

Some widows wind up going off the charts, spending on themselves and their children soon after their partner's death because they think it helps them ease their grief or because they have large cash inflows from life insurance death benefits.

Organize your financial documents. Draw up a list of your household's bank accounts, brokerage accounts, retirement plans, insurance policies, loans, credit card statements, and mortgages and get the most recent statements for them. Then, you'll be able to begin taking necessary notification actions with your partner's bank, brokerage, and other financial institutions.

You'll also need to locate copies of your joint tax returns for the past five years and your marriage certificate.

File insurance claims. File a claim with your partner's life insurance company. Your partner's insurance agent should have applicable policy information and can help you get the necessary forms. Or, you can send a letter to the insurance company, including a copy of the death certificate and your partner's policy number, requesting the forms necessary to file a claim. You can choose to receive the money as a lump payment or in installments over a certain period.

Many widows I have spoken to wish they had not taken lump-sum payouts and put the proceeds in an easy-to-dip-into account. One solution is to take the lump-sum, but ask your planner to set it up to dole the funds out in smaller monthly increments to prevent it from slipping through your hands too quickly.

Contact government offices. Contact your state's office to inquire about inheritance tax. Change the title and registration of any cars or trucks listed in your partner's name by contacting your local department of motor vehicles. You'll want the registration in your name when you sell the car.

Notify the Social Security Administration (ssa.gov). You can also call the SSA at 800-772-1213, or go to a local office to sign a claim form for survivors' benefits. You must have been married at least for nine months prior to your partner's death to be eligible for benefits. You can receive reduced benefits as early as age 60 or full benefits at full retirement age or older.

You will need both your partner's and your birth certificates, your Social Security numbers, and your marriage certificate. If you have dependent children, you'll also need their birth certificates and Social Security numbers. You must also produce your partner's W-2 forms for the past two years if he/she was still working at the time of death.

If you feel up to it, you might want to check on your own Social Security benefits at the same time to be sure your benefits are accruing properly. You can set up a "My Social Security" account at its website, ssa.gov/myaccount. You can use the Social Security Administration's online retirement estimator to get an idea of what your future benefits might be. You can also correct any mistakes and be sure they have accurate data about your earnings history.

Your survivor benefit amount is based on the earnings of the person who died. The more he or she paid into Social Security, the higher your benefits would be. If you remarry after you reach age sixty (age fifty if disabled), your remarriage will not affect your eligibility for survivors' benefits. For details, go to the Social Security Survivors Planner at ssa.gov/planners/survivors.

If your partner was a veteran, contact the Department of Veterans Affairs. You may be eligible for a pension of some sort. You can apply for Survivors Pension by downloading and mailing the completed form to your local regional benefit office or by visiting your local office (benefits.va.gov/pension/spousepen.asp). This agency might pay several hundred dollars toward burial and funeral expenses. For more details, go to benefits.va.gov/compensation/claims-special-burial.asp.

Contact financial services providers. Meet with your bank manager. If your partner had an account in his or her name alone, it should be changed to an account called "Estate of." You'll need your partner's Social Security number to secure an estate tax ID number, which you can then use as the account number. Deposit all income from your partner's assets under the new number, and pay any estate administration expenses (such as the funeral cost) from this account. Any joint accounts should be transferred to an account in your name. You'll need a copy of the death certificate to do so. As for outstanding checks, you can decide to honor them or not. Then, too, you might be able to renegotiate the terms of any outstanding loans with your banker.

Contact your stockbroker or financial advisor and ask for the necessary paperwork to change the accounts to either your name or the estate's account. To change the name on a joint account, you'll need to show a copy of the death certificate, an affidavit of domicile (the stockbroker has this), and a letter of request with your Social Security number. Ask your broker or advisor to give you a value on the assets in your partner's accounts and your joint accounts at the time of his or her death. Your estate taxes will be based on that valuation.

TAX TIPS

Marital deduction. You can avoid estate tax altogether if your partner has left everything to you (provided you are a U.S. citizen). Under the unlimited marital deduction, any assets you inherit directly from your partner, such as life insurance benefits, certificates of deposit, or bank accounts, are not subject to federal income tax.

Federal estate and gift taxes, called the unified gift and estate tax. For deaths occurring in 2017, someone can leave or give away up to $5.49 million, total, before taxes are levied. It doesn't matter who inherits it. This is known as the personal estate tax exemption. The amount is indexed for inflation. If the estate is worth less than the exemption amount, no federal estate tax is due.

Charitable deductions. All property left to a tax-exempt charity is free of estate tax.

State estate taxes. Even if your estate isn't big enough to owe federal estate tax, your state may still collect its own estate or inheritance taxes.

Inheritance. When you inherit a home or investments such as stocks and bonds, you pay tax only when you sell and only on the growth after you inherited it.

Deceased's tax return. An annual tax return must be filed for the earnings and investment income that your partner accumulated up to the date he or she died. The return for that year must be filed with the Internal Revenue Service by April 15 of the following year. Usually, the executor of the estate is responsible for filing it; if not, you are responsible for filing. The form is the same as if your partner were still living, but the word "deceased" must be typed after his or her name, along with the date of death.

Joint tax return. You may file a joint tax return for the year in which your partner dies and pay under that tax rate. On the line where you sign the return, you must indicate in writing that you are filing as a surviving partner. The following year, you may file as either a single taxpayer or a surviving partner. The tax tables for each differ.

Refunds. For a refund, you'll need to file a separate form, called Form 1310, "Statement of a Person Claiming Refund Due a Deceased Taxpayer."

Health deductions. You should deduct all the medical bills incurred by your partner during the year in which he or she died, even if you don't pay them until up to twelve months later.

ROUND TWO: UPDATE YOUR INSURANCE

After you've made it through that first rigorous to-do list, give yourself a well-deserved break, then gear up for the next set of money matters. These steps should be handled before too much time passes, although not necessarily in the first few weeks.

Update your health insurance. Under the Consolidated Omnibus Budget Reconciliation Act, or COBRA, former partners can purchase an extension of their ex's employer coverage for up to thirty-six months. You must notify the plan administrator within thirty days of your spouse's death to qualify, though.

But be forewarned: COBRA premiums are lofty. You pay the full price of your partner's plan, including the portion that his or her employer was paying, plus a 2 percent administration fee. There's no choice of plans—you keep the same plan you two already had with the employer.

COBRA generally applies to group health plans offered by employers with twenty or more employees. Many states offer mini-COBRA benefits, which apply to employers with two to nineteen employees. The length of coverage ranges from three months to thirty-six months, depending on the state. Your state insurance department's site will note if residents are eligible for mini-COBRA benefits.

If this is not an option, you might be able to switch to your own employer's plan, if there is one, or sign up for a group policy though your union, an association, or a religious group that you belong to. If you are a real estate agent, for example, contact the local realtor trade association.

Some groups, like bar associations, churches, and alumni associations, offer their members discounted health insurance. If you run a small business and belong to the local chamber of commerce, you might be able to tap into its favorable group rates. The National Association for the Self-Employed offers insurance, too, as does the Freelancers Union.

Compare single plans available in your area at the federal website Healthcare.gov. Check your state insurance department website, too, since it might list health insurance choices for residents. Also, be sure to ask your doctors which insurance carriers they accept.

If you'll be shopping for an individual health policy, compare premiums, deductibles, and out-of-pocket expenses. Always check to see if your preferred doctors are "in-network" before you select a plan. Expect to pay an annual deductible of $1,000, $2,500 or even $5,000 to keep your premium costs down.

You also can get a local health insurance agent to shop around on your behalf. Look for one at the National Association of Health Underwriters website (nahu.org).

Consider opening a Health Savings Account (HSA). These accounts must be paired with an eligible high-deductible health insurance plan. The money you put into the accounts is tax-free: either your employer takes it out before taxes are assessed, or you can deduct the amount from your tax return if the account is held at a bank or other institution that is not affiliated with your employer. It grows tax-free and is tax-free when used for health-related qualified medical expenses for you, your partner or a qualified dependent. These expenses include deductibles, copays and coinsurance, and prescription drugs, plus other qualified medical expenses not covered by your plan. Insurance premiums, however, usually cannot be paid with HSA funds.

In addition, any withdrawals for nonqualified expenses will be subject to income tax and may be subject to an additional 20 percent tax. Not sure if your insurance plan is considered high-deductible? A good place to start is asking HR or your plan administrator.

Your HSA balance rolls over from year to year, so the earlier you start, the better, because you give your money more time to grow tax-free. HSAs can be invested in mutual funds, stocks, and other investments. However, investment choices may be limited to those options being offered by the bank or institution where your HSA is held. If your goal is to use the money for retirement healthcare expenses, make sure to invest some of it in stocks that can typically beat inflation over the long haul. That's good news.

You don't have to invest in individual stocks. You might consider buying a Standard & Poor's 500 index fund, an exchange-traded fund that tracks the S&P 500 or a total U.S. stock market index fund. S&P 500 stocks also pay dividends. So unlike bonds, they can potentially offer a double payday: they provide income with cash dividends and there's the strong potential for capital appreciation, based on the historical performance of the stock market. (Please keep in mind, however, past performance is not a guaranteed indicator of future performance.)

Once you've hit age sixty-five and enroll in Medicare, you can no longer contribute to an HSA, but you can still use the money for out-of-pocket qualified medical expenses. In the meantime, there are no minimum required distributions at 70½ like other retirement accounts, and you can leave any remaining funds after you die to a named beneficiary. The money you put into an HSA doesn't affect the contribution limits in place for IRAs, so you could potentially see this as another way to save for retirement, with medical care in mind, specifically. Ask your tax professional for details, including contribution limits. You can also search for specific details on IRS.gov.

HSA ADVANTAGES

- ☝ Money goes in pretax or contributions are tax-deductible.
- ☝ Money grows tax-free in account.
- ☝ Money can be withdrawn tax-free to cover qualified medical expenses.

The buildup is tax-free, so whatever earnings you get on the account—whether it's interest earnings or if you invest the money in stocks or mutual funds or some type of brokerage account—accrue tax-free, and when money comes out for qualified medical expenses, it's tax-free.

HSA DISADVANTAGES

- ☝ Withdrawals used for nonqualified medical expenses before someone becomes eligible for Medicare are subject to income taxes and a 20 percent penalty.
- ☝ After you enroll in Medicare at age sixty-five, withdrawals for nonmedical expenses are not subject to the 20 percent penalty, although they are subject to income taxes, similar to a traditional IRA, and will have benefited from years or decades of tax deferral.
- ☝ Contributions to the account can be made only up until an individual enrolls in Medicare as the primary source of insurance.

Your contributions can be used tax-free for medical expenses in any year. In 2017, if you have an HSA–eligible health insurance policy—with a deductible of at least $1,300

(or $2,600 for family coverage)—you can contribute up to
$3,400 to an HSA (or $6,750 for family coverage), plus $1,000
if you're fifty-five or older.

To find one and compare fees, go to hsasearch.com.

Update your disability insurance. You might already have
some disability insurance (which pays benefits if you are
unable to work) from your employer, but it probably isn't going
to be enough. Most employer plans cover just 50 percent to 70
percent of your annual income. In fact, only about one-third of
big U.S. employers provide any coverage at all. Some states,
including New York and California, require employers to offer
short-term disability insurance that might last up to six months.

But without the benefit of a second income to fall back on
if something happens to you either physically or emotionally
to prevent you from working, you'll need to boost that
coverage. Claire, for instance, went back to work 10 days
after her husband's death. Six months later, she fell into deep
depression and was out of work for seven weeks.

For a policy that will replace 60 percent of your income,
expect to pay 2 percent of your salary. You can lower that
amount by opting for a longer waiting period (say, thirty to
ninety days) before benefits kick in.

Review your life insurance needs. Life insurance should be
taken care of in a speedy fashion only if you have dependents.
If you're widowed with dependent kids, you might want to buy
extra insurance since you are now your children's only means
of support. If you are a single mother, ask yourself how long
your children will need your financial support. How much life
insurance you need depends on how many children you have
and how old they are. One guideline suggested by financial

planners is to buy coverage worth about eight to ten times your annual salary.

Life insurance generally is available in two forms, term or cash value.

Term insurance is the simplest and most affordable life insurance to buy if you plan to insure yourself for at least twenty years. You pay an annual premium based on your age, your health, the agent's commission, and how much the insurer thinks it can earn by investing your premium until you die. Term is usually the least expensive form of life insurance you can buy. Term insurance pays a specific death benefit to your survivors.

The other form of life insurance, called **cash value insurance**, is a combination of a life policy and a savings plan. There are several types of these policies. The most common are whole life, universal life, and variable life.

Whole life invests your money mostly in bonds, and you get a fixed return and a traditional death benefit.

Universal life lets you decide how much you want to pay in premiums and sets the death benefit accordingly. Universal life, unlike whole life, offers a variable interest rate that depends on the current market rate. The amount of your funds that exceeds the annual premium cost is invested for you and is tax-deferred.

Variable life invests money in a choice of stocks, bonds, and money market funds. The growth is tax-deferred until withdrawn. A portion of the money pays for your annual premiums.

Women who make more than $100,000 and want around $700,000 in coverage might shop for a cash value policy.

Bankrate's life insurance calculator can be a good place to start to determine which option is best for you: bankrate.com/calculators/insurance/life-insurance-calculator.aspx

Keep in mind, though, if you liquidate your cash life insurance policy during the first couple of years, you will lose all your investment. Typically, it takes five years for cash value policyholders to see any returns. The Consumer Federation of America (CFA) advises that you steer clear of such a policy unless you can keep it at least for twenty years. That lets the cash value portion of the policy build. About one-quarter of such consumers, however, stop paying into the policies after three years.

The rates of return on cash life insurance policies vary widely from year to year and from policy to policy. The policies are terribly complex, and many agents are unable to explain them properly to consumers. But you can have specific cash value policies analyzed by using CFA's Life Insurance Rate of Return Service, which estimates true investment returns on any cash value life insurance policy. Call CFA at 202-387-0087 (or go to evaluatelifeinsurance.org) for more information about this service, which costs $125 for the first example.

- Check out insurance firms, like USAA Life (USAA.com) or Ameritas (ameritas.com), that sell policies directly to you without going through an agent.
- Standard & Poor's (standardandpoors.com), Morningstar (morningstar.com), and Weiss Research (800-289-9222) rate the insurers for financial soundness.

When hiring an insurance agent, look for reputable designations like Chartered Financial Consultant (ChFC) and Charted Life Underwriter (CLU), both awarded by the American College of Financial Services in Bryn Mawr, Pennsylvania, the insurance and financial industry's stellar institution of higher learning.

Put together your own board of directors. As I mentioned, you are not looking to hook up with some stock jockey for investments. The goal is to find someone you feel comfortable with who can help you get your finances in order and start you on the road to educating yourself about money.

You'll want to set up appointments with your attorney and accountant if you have them. If not, ask for recommendations and seek to hire your own. You may need to interview a few until you find one who's a good match.

A financial planner is another good resource for some advice on how to invest any insurance payout. You might interview several advisors at different financial services providers. It's a process.

The best way to get this kind of search started is to ask for references from friends or relatives. Your partner may already have a relationship with a firm, while you had other financial services firms in your wheelhouse. Diligently interview them all.

Ask tough questions until you are satisfied. Approach the task as if you are an employer interviewing someone for a job. Look for candid answers to your questions. For example, there is nothing wrong with asking a prospective advisor how he or she defines success with a client. Is it a certain rate of return for a portfolio? Or helping a client save for a certain life goal, say, a home, or college education for a child?

Listen to their answers. You want to work with an advisor who isn't only focused on the family's assets, but one who has a more holistic approach regarding getting to know more about you, your family, your goals, and risk tolerance. Your goal is to build a relationship with a person or firm that can make your overall financial life smoother and provide the needed ballast of a team of specialists when necessary, say, an attorney who could help with estate planning questions.

In the next chapter, I'll discuss what you need to do at once if you think your marriage is in jeopardy, or if you are separated, and what can wait. Some of the advice is not so different from what widows need to do, but the approach is quite different and the obstacles a bit trickier to navigate since this is about dividing assets. But if you are confident, you'll get through it with a minimal amount of emotional and financial scarring.

CHAPTER RECAP

In this chapter, we discussed:

- Finding a support group
- Locating your partner's important documents
- Contacting his or her advisors
- First action steps, such as paying immediate bills and obtaining death certificates
- Exploring tax implications
- Contacting government agencies
- Updating your own insurance needs
- Building your own board of directors

CHAPTER THREE

THINGS TO DO IF YOUR MARRIAGE IS IN JEOPARDY

Women whose partners die may have had little warning or time to prepare to take charge of their financial affairs. But if your marriage is heading for divorce, you can get your act together ahead of time. You just have to make the right moves early on. For most of you, the biggest problem is going to be a psychological one—overcoming denial.

If you're like Melissa, whose husband left her for another woman, you probably think you can win your partner back. You convince yourself that this is just a temporary situation and cling to the hope that everything will work out in time. You go to counseling sessions and hope that everything will return to normal. You delude yourself into thinking that a few months of separation will give your partner time to have the fling and be done with it. Or perhaps, you fall for your partner's tale of financial troubles and don't fight for what's rightfully yours. Empathy will get you nowhere.

Of course, it's not that you're simply naive. This reaction is perfectly natural. You want to believe the person you've spent years of your life living with, side-by-side, day-by-day, wouldn't really want to harm you. Down deep there's a layer of trust that makes you unable to fathom that the marriage is

39

over, or that your partner would deny you and your child or children the support you deserve.

So you do nothing but wait and worry and feel rejected and lousy about yourself and, understandably, angry with your partner. But worst of all, you refuse to deal with the key money issues; you freeze. If you want to become a money-confident woman, get it together.

Once the love is gone, money is the issue, the *only* issue. It's what will help you live through the upheaval and start over. You must be coldhearted. Maybe that's not attractive, but it's survival at this point.

Of course, an initial separation doesn't mean your marriage is over. Reconciliation is always possible. But the fact is, your partner might decide not to try to get the marriage back on track, period. Then again, he or she might want to come back, sheepishly begging for forgiveness, but *you've* already tossed in the towel and moved on with your life.

The fact is that roughly four out of ten marriages today end in divorce. While that's down from 50 percent a decade ago, it's still significant. Meanwhile, the National Center for Family & Marriage Research says the divorce rate among adults fifty and older has been multiplying. Untangling your personal life from that of your partner's is going to be wrenching. Untangling your *finances* from those of your soon-to-be ex-partner is likely to be super difficult.

Don't count on alimony from your partner to bail you out while you struggle for financial freedom. Alimony, once a standard "gift" from an ex, has become a relic of the past, as more women have accumulated their own assets during marriage through their careers and, possibly, inheritances. Even if you have the option, say, of being out of the workforce to raise a family or for caregiving, and can argue that you need the financial support, alimony typically lasts just a handful of years. In some states, alimony is provided only if the marriage lasted at least ten years. Accepting a lump sum of money as part of a divorce settlement is probably better than agreeing to alimony payments anyway. It's a bird in hand, so to speak.

Here's what you need to do first if your marriage is on the verge of collapsing.

CALL AN ATTORNEY

Even if things are just starting to get rocky, you need to get some advice from an impartial outsider. These are highly emotional times, and a friend's advice just won't cut it now. This is a matrimonial battlefield, and you've got to look out for yourself. That's especially true if you have children.

Just going for a consultation doesn't mean you've set in motion a course that can't be reversed. It just makes good sense to hire someone who can help you evaluate your assets and press for the best possible settlement. You need to know how long the divorce proceedings will take. Each state has its own requirements for length of separation before divorce. How much are you going to need to live on during that time?

Ask your recently divorced friends and colleagues for recommendations. A tax or estate attorney can also provide a referral. You want to be sure the attorney you choose is someone who specializes in matrimonial law. Moreover, avoid using the same attorney your partner uses, or even asking for a referral from an accountant who currently works with both of you. It seems obvious, but often, especially when a divorce isn't a bitter one, couples opt to save money by having one lawyer do it all. Forget that. You want someone looking out for *your* best interests, not someone whose job is to make sure the divorce is pushed through smoothly and cheaply.

Use your lawyer's time wisely. When you are paying anywhere from $200 to $600 an hour for legal counsel, you want concrete discussions about your *finances,* not about your emotional distress. See a therapist to help you deal with those personal feelings. This negotiation is about cold cash.

DO-IT-YOURSELF DIVORCES

You might be able to skip attorney fees if you and your partner have just a handful of assets, have been married a relatively short time, have no children, and have hardly any debt. These do-it-yourself divorces can be executed by calling your local divorce court and requesting the correct form. Again, this process will be dependent on state statutes for necessary length of separation.

Most county clerks' offices provide some of the basic information required when filing your own divorce. (Sometimes this is available at your county clerk's website, so check there first.) If you want to find information about where your local court is, which branch you should use, filing fees, or clerk's hours, you can usually find a direct link to the court website at statelocalgov.net or ncsc.org. You can also get a paralegal to help, or check out web-based divorce services at divorcenet. com.

MEDIATION

Mediation is an option and is generally less expensive than a standard litigated divorce and faster. Although the process differs from state to state, the idea is that you and your soon-to-be ex hire someone who is a professional divorce mediator to work out an agreement that is fair to both of you. The hourly sessions usually cost between $100 to $200 and might involve several sessions. It's often a good idea to hire a divorce mediator who agrees to a flat fee for all services that comprise a comprehensive marital estate assessment.

Your chief concern is to select a mediator who is neutral and not an advocate either for you or your partner. You will need to consult with your own attorneys prior to signing the final divorce settlement agreement and have him or her review the final agreement, then file it in your local divorce court. Mediation generally works only if you know the total value of all your assets and where they are located.

The upside to mediation is that it's private versus public, if you decide to litigate in court. The potential downside is, since all financial information is willingly revealed, in other words, voluntarily, your partner could hypothetically conceal assets or sources of income. The mediator's job is *not* to give you any advice. The mediator is solely there to get you two to agree on your terms. One final note: If one partner is controlling and domineering and the other is more deferential by nature (and that could be you), the final settlement may turn out lopsided in the more controlling partner's favor. It seems like a kinder, gentler option, but a high degree of trust and honesty is required. For many couples, those characteristics have sailed a long time ago.

COLLABORATIVE DIVORCE

No one really wants to drag all their business out in a public court and leave it to a judge to decide their fate. A so-called "collaborative" divorce has a certain appeal to it.

With a collaborative divorce, each partner hires an attorney who specializes in this type of process. Each attorney, then, helps his or her client drill down to an agreement. It's a dance. You meet with your respective lawyers, then you all meet together. There might be a therapist who helps you work through the emotions of custody or other hot-button issues that have nothing to do with money.

If it all goes kaput, you have to start all over again with new counsel. Speed can give this path a thumbs-up, if that's what you want, and sure, it can be much less expensive than traditional divorce litigation. But be forewarned, if your situation is thorny at all and there are sizable assets, it's possible that lots of financial information will never see the light of day.

Like mediation, all disclosure is voluntary. If you are the least bit worried that you're unsure of where the financial pieces are and have let your partner control most of the money decisions, I would steer you away from this kind of process. Hiding assets and income is oh, so easy to do. This is a time when suspicious minds must be on high alert. Laurie's husband was adamant that they go this route, but she knew better having seen her husband lie repeatedly throughout their lives together to friends, clients, and family maintaining a poker face; she stood her ground.

Other reasons these faster, cheaper options should be avoided are in situations where your partner is overbearing and you really have trouble standing up to him or her. Another reason to put the kibosh on one of these quicker solutions is if there has been any, and I mean even a *whisper*, of domestic violence in your time together, even if you have never breathed a word of it to anyone. Finally, if your partner has any history of substance abuse issues, that's a warning to go another route. All these situations create a possibility that nothing collaborative will come of this procedure.

TRADITIONAL DIVORCE

This is the basic model. And even though they're called "litigated," most divorce cases are settled well before they land in court.

The most important and most difficult parts of any divorce are coming to an agreement on child custody, division of assets and liabilities, and alimony payments (how much and for how long). The key to success is to be reasonable.

If it does wind up in court, believe me, it can get ugly. But sometimes that's the only way to get what's fair, so be prepared and put on your big girl pants. Once it hits the courtroom, a judge will have the final say about everything from the children to how the assets are divvied up.

LEARN THE THREE BASIC ELEMENTS OF DIVORCE

To fully take advantage of applicable laws, you should become familiar with three important factors: alimony, child support, and division of property.

Alimony

Regardless of where you live, if alimony is awarded, a partner usually has to deliver financial support to an ex-partner for a narrow window of time, usually two to five years. Alimony is ordered by a court on the basis of one partner's need or entitlement and the other partner's ability to pay. Alimony is taxable to the partner who receives it and is a tax deduction for the partner who pays.

Child Support

Every state has its own rules for figuring out the appropriate amount of child support for divorcing parents. Depending on your state, child-support payments usually last until the youngest child is eighteen. These payments are not taxable. You can get a copy of your state's support formula from your attorney or a clerk in the divorce court.

If you have a child whom you expect to be college-bound, write an agreement plainly stating who will pay for the child's college education. Also, if you are to receive child-support payments, insist that the paying partner purchase a life insurance policy covering the term of the payments, naming you as the owner and beneficiary of the policy. Your ex-partner will also be unable to change the beneficiary without your agreement.

Division of Property in Your State

Here are the three basic definitions:

Community property. All the property and assets accumulated during your marriage are considered to be community property, which is divided equally between the divorcing parties. Property acquired before the marriage and inherited property are excluded. The community-property states currently are Arizona, California, Idaho, Louisiana, Nevada, New Mexico, Texas, Washington, and Wisconsin.

Common-law property. Property divided according to who holds the title to the asset is considered common-law property.

Equitable distribution. This is the basic method of distributing property in the remaining states plus the District of Columbia.

The court decides how to divide the assets based on criteria such as need, earnings potential, and financial contribution to the marriage. Keep in mind that *equitable* does not always mean *fair*.

ESTABLISH YOUR OWN CREDIT

It's critical to establish your own **credit record**. Before you make any sudden moves, you'll want to make certain that you have a credit history in your name alone. If you do not have a credit card, apply for one immediately, before you agree to separate. Even in today's marriages, women who may have been supporting themselves for a decade or so before marrying buy into this idea of holding joint credit cards with their partner.

Married couples frequently cancel credit cards held prior to the marriage and carry jointly-held ones only. Their argument is that you should share everything. Some partners may be afraid you will somehow use this to hide your spending. It can be a trust issue, while women see it as one of control. Every woman needs a Visa or MasterCard in her own name. (Note that Amex has to be paid off each month, so it doesn't indicate an ability to manage revolving debt, and department store cards cards tend to have less stringent underwriting standards than those of traditional credit cards, so they aren't as valued in credit scoring models.) It's important not only to have your own line of credit, but also to build a solid credit record by paying off the balance regularly and on time. A healthy credit history is worth its weight in gold at this stage in your life.

After you have your own credit in place, **close all joint credit card accounts**. Inform credit companies in writing that you want the accounts closed and will not be responsible for any charges from that time on. Request an accounting of outstanding charges. You can either pay them off yourself or make a deal with your ex. The balance must be paid off before they will close the account.

Notify all other creditors of your change in status if you are divorcing. This means contacting your mortgage holder, bank loan officer, and any other credit card companies.

Your bank is the next stop. **If you don't already have checking and savings accounts in your name, open them.** Again, this notion of separating money in a marriage is usually pretty emotional. The thinking is that it is all "our" money. This can be a major mistake when you are in the throes of a divorce. You've got to separate your money quickly and cleanly. It just gets messy when it is all pooled together.

In general, women who are separated but not yet divorced should close any joint bank accounts. In some cases, though, you might want to keep the joint account open temporarily to pay for household expenses until the settlement is final. If that's the case, ask the bank to freeze the account. That way both your signature and your partner's are required before any transaction can be made.

If you have any joint brokerage accounts, write at once and notify them that you are separated from your partner. Ask the broker not to make any transactions without your approval. If you have a **margin account** that lets you borrow money from the brokerage to make other investments, this step is critical. You don't want your partner investing with that borrowed money because you'll be liable not only for the loan, but the interest as well. That's especially troubling if the investment goes south.

DETERMINE YOUR NET WORTH

Find out just what you're worth. By putting a dollar amount on what you own **(assets)** and what you owe **(liabilities)**, you can calculate your **net worth** (assets minus liabilities). You may think you know what your assets are, but don't assume so. Your partner may hold properties or investments about which you are clueless. You may not even have the correct information about his or her pension or pensions if he or she has worked for several employers over the course of a career. A hard-nosed assessment of your financial situation is crucial.

Even in the best of unions, it's a good idea to check up on how your partnership is faring financially on an annual basis. However, if you haven't done so and are heading for a separation, do so at once. For pension and retirement plan sums, call your employer's benefit departments. You may not be able to get this from your partner's employer, but potentially you will find this documentation in household files. This is all information that you are entitled to know, so be persistent.

You might not be able to get the precise value for all your assets, but do your best to track down an approximate value. Hire an appraiser, if need be, to get a realistic value on your furnishings, jewelry, and collectibles. Check out the contents of any safe-deposit box, and make sure you haven't missed any deeds or documents that will add to your list. Your tax return from last year will help identify any assets you may have forgotten to include. For those of you who are really having trouble gathering the numbers, you should call your accountant or insurance agent.

It's fairly easy to track down those to whom you owe money, but if there's a problem, call each credit card issuer, your mortgage holder, and other creditors to get an up-to-date accounting. Visit annualcreditreport.com to request a free credit report from the three major consumer credit reporting agencies—Experian, Equifax, and TransUnion. They can give you a copy of your credit report, which will list all your creditors. You might even turn up a credit card or two that your partner has been carrying without your knowledge. Once your divorce is final, inform the credit bureaus in writing of your new status.

Use this chart as a model to keep track of your net worth.

Liabilities	Quantity
Mortgage	
Home Equity Loan	
Other Property Loans	
Car Loans	
College Loans	
Credit Card Debt	
Other Loans	
TOTAL DEBT	
Assets	
Less Debts	
TOTAL (YOUR HOUSEHOLD NET WORTH)	

INCOME AND BUDGETING

Now you'll want to take some time to review your sources of income. Will you need to find another job that pays more in order to support yourself? What can you afford to pay for living expenses such as rent or a mortgage? Will you need to ask your partner for financial support? Will he or she ask you for it? With women moving into higher-ranked corporate positions, their salaries have risen accordingly. Today, some women earn as much or more than their partners do. Then, too, you may have inherited money, and he or she may want a portion of that as well. Either way, knowing what you have coming in is essential to putting together a financial plan.

You'll want to establish a monthly budget early on that works for you. You should plan to set aside an emergency fund. Most advisors suggest you set aside six months of living expenses; if you can gradually build up to a year's worth, do. A money market mutual fund or a bank savings account are smart, safe places to stockpile this money.

Devising a budget that will let you live within your means is essential. Moreover, if you are going to be requesting alimony, you will need to show documentation for your monthly output over a period of time to establish need. You'll probably have to cut back on spending until you get your finances on solid ground. We will discuss how to outline a budget in the next chapter.

UPDATE YOUR INSURANCE

Typical divorce settlements specify that the children are beneficiaries of your ex-partner's life insurance. But you'll want to quickly change the beneficiary on your own current life insurance. It's essential to insure your life even if your partner is covering your children. Refer to Chapter Two for advice on how to shop for several types of insurance, including life, health, and disability. As with widowed women, COBRA laws dictate that if you are covered by your partner's company plan, you should be able to continue the same health coverage for at least thirty-six months, but you will be responsible for paying the premiums. After that, it's up to you to find a comprehensive policy that is affordable.

DECISIONS THAT WILL AFFECT YOUR
FINANCIAL WELL-BEING

You'll be called upon to make some decisions that will affect your future financial health.

What to Do with the House?

Consider selling the house. For some reason, we all want to hang on to the house. Although it represents stability and the memories of happier times, it's also an incredible financial drain for someone living on one income. It provides zero income. There are monthly mortgage payments, home maintenance, and thousands of dollars in annual property taxes and insurance that crop up month after month. For divorcees, selling the house and splitting the proceeds with your ex is usually the best way to go. Then you can rent or buy a smaller place.

Go for the Pension

As a divorced partner, you are typically entitled to a portion of any retirement benefits earned by your ex during your marriage. In order to get a cut of that retirement plan—either a pension, a 401(k), or an IRA—you'll need a lawyer to petition a state court for a **qualified domestic relations order**, or QDRO (pronounced "quadro"), for a judge to approve. This is an order from the court that explains to a pension plan administrator how to divide the benefits between yourself and your partner.

There are several options, including a one-time payment, monthly payouts at retirement, or a lump-sum payment that you transfer directly into your own IRA, where your money will continue to grow tax-free until you begin withdrawals, which are mandatory at age 70½.

Divorcing women often pass up their soon-to-be ex's pension in favor of the house or upfront cash they can use today. But someone earning around $70,000 a year today could easily retire with a lifetime pension of $1 million or more, depending on the number of years he or she has paid in.

Don't raid your ex's retirement funds. Experts advise you roll over directly into an IRA any employer-sponsored retirement funds you receive in the settlement rather than cashing out the money. By law, however, you're allowed to withdraw money from your ex's 401(k) or 403(b) plan one time without incurring the 10 percent early withdrawal tax penalty if you're under age 59½. If you're buried with legal fees, you may want to pull out a fraction of the retirement funds to pay for them. But keep withdrawals to a minimum; you want the money in the retirement funds to continue growing tax-deferred until you truly need it down the road at retirement.

If your partner has a Roth IRA or Roth 401(k), go for that before his or her standard 401(k) or traditional IRA. With a 401(k) or traditional IRA, you'll be taxed when you withdraw money in retirement. With a Roth IRA or Roth 401(k), however, the earnings won't be taxed, since that plan was funded with after-tax dollars.

Timing

As devious as it sounds, it pays to time your divorce well to maximize your financial position. As long as you have been married at least 10 years and don't remarry, you can qualify for Social Security benefits based on your ex-partner's earnings when you both reach age sixty-two, even if he or she has remarried or hasn't yet retired and begun to receive benefits.

The rules do say that your Social Security benefits based on your own work history must be less than half of your ex-partner's benefits at age sixty-five. You must also have been divorced for at least two years to make a claim. So try to drag out the marriage for at least ten years—even if he or she wants out after 9½ years. And remember, even if you are on decent terms with your ex-partner when the time comes, you should plan to collect this benefit. Doing so won't reduce his or her payout at all, and they'll never even know when you start receiving Social Security checks.

TAX TIPS

- You should file your income tax to the IRS as **single** (not as married filing jointly) if your divorce is finalized by year-end.
- Part of your attorney's fees might be tax-deductible, so keep an itemized record of your bills. This is typically possible for any tax advice they gave you.
- Should your partner agree to provide alimony payments or money to maintain your home and life each month, you'll probably be required to pay taxes on that income. Those payments, however, are tax-deductible for your former partner.
- The ex may agree not to call the payments "alimony." In that case, you avoid taxes, but the

ex misses the deduction. To get your ex to agree, you might be able to compromise on a smaller amount so you'll both benefit.

- Alimony income may be considered as "earned income" to you. If so, it may be eligible for contributions to an IRA.
- Since there are no taxes taken out of those alimony checks, you probably will have to file quarterly tax returns on the funds. Your accountant can estimate that amount for you and provide you with the correct forms.
- If you have children, you may qualify for head-of-household status and be eligible to use the dependent exemption, thereby cutting your tax bite. You have to be named as the custodial parent in the divorce decree to do so.
- Child support is not taxed as income, nor can your ex deduct it.
- You may be eligible for the "Child and Dependent Care Credit" as well. Childcare includes daycare, nursery school, and even kindergarten. The amount of your credit is between 20 to 35 percent of your allowable expenses. The percentage you use depends on the amount of your adjusted gross income. Your credit is determined by the amount you pay for childcare and your **adjusted gross income** (income on which your federal taxes are computed). In general, if you have one child under the age of thirteen in day care, the first $3,000 you spend qualifies. If you have two or more children under that age in daycare, the first $6,000 qualifies. The total credit drops, though, as

your income rises. For more details, go to the IRS.
gov website.

- All dependent children must have a Social
  Security number for you to claim them as a
  dependent.

- Check with your employer to see if there is a
  dependent care flexible spending account. Some
  employers allow you to set aside as much as
  $5,000 from your annual pretax income to pay for
  childcare.

- The sum set aside in a reimbursement plan will
  reduce the amount you can apply for as childcare
  credit. For most people, the reimbursement
  account is usually the best bet.

- If you decide to keep the house, you won't pay
  taxes at the time of your divorce settlement, but
  it may be subject to taxes should you sell it down
  the road. That can be a serious blow, because
  you pay taxes on all the appreciation before it
  was transferred to your sole ownership and after.
  Currently, if you owned and lived in the place for
  two of the five years before the sale, then up to
  $250,000 of profit is tax-free. If you are married
  and file a joint return, the tax-free amount doubles
  to $500,000. The law lets you "exclude" this
  amount of otherwise taxable profit from your
  taxable income. Meantime, there's no limit on
  the number of times you can use the home-sale
  exemption. In most cases, you can make tax-free
  profits of $250,000, or $500,000 depending on
  your filing status, every time you sell a home.
  A **capital gain or loss** is the amount you make

or lose when you sell an asset like a home. Documentation is important for tax purposes.

GETTING FINANCIAL ADVICE

Take your time before making major investment decisions with your settlement money. There are all sorts of people out there ready to pounce on your money for their gain, not yours. It's best to let your head clear for a few months before making any major investment decisions. Instead, set the funds aside in certificates of deposit or money market accounts. Even though these accounts pay low interest, they are a safe and relatively liquid place to keep your money while you get up to speed in the world of investing. To compare rates on CDs and money market accounts, check out Bankrate.com.

Seek financial advice before you agree to terms of a settlement. A good financial planner can help you sort things out without pushing you to make fast decisions about how to invest your settlement money. If you don't already have a financial planner whom you trust, you might want to check around with some friends or relatives to see if they have any good recommendations. For unbiased guidance, look for a fee-only planner with the Certified Financial Planner designation. You can find one by visiting sites of the National Association of Personal Financial Advisors (Napfa.org), the Financial Planning Association (onefpa.org), and the Certified Financial Planner Board of Standards (cfp.net). (But don't expect the planner to make your decisions for you. You are solely responsible for your choices now. In Chapter Five, we will discuss in more detail how to choose a financial planner.)

Hire a good accountant. Divorce and taxes can be messy. An accountant is one professional you would be well-advised to have on board before you agree to any final terms of the divorce.

It's understandable if all this seems like more than you can handle, so take it easy and go one step at a time. In the next chapter, we'll show you how to develop a budget that works for you.

CHAPTER RECAP

In this chapter, we discussed:

- Different types of divorce
- Income and budgeting
- Timing your divorce
- Getting financial advice
- Tax tips

CHAPTER FOUR

DEVISE A BUDGET THAT WORKS

Finding the essential papers and taking those first steps toward financial independence are difficult chores at best. Money issues are such a distant second to your emotional stress right now. Unfortunately, this is the time you must press ahead. In the end, you'll be grateful you did. Developing a sensible, personally customized budget will allow you to take control of your spending and make your financial life secure.

Don't be surprised, though, if for the first six months or so your monthly spending and budgeting is all over the map. Eventually, things will settle into place and it will be easier to anticipate your monthly spending and saving needs.

You've already assembled the most important documents and set up shop in your makeshift office. Laid out in front of you is the data that will help you put your budget together. Essentially, you must determine how to allocate your incoming funds to satisfy your spending needs while continuing to protect and build your nest egg for your retirement, for your children's education, to support elderly parents, or other future money demands.

The most important thing to remember is that this is not a time to be careless with your funds or to hand over all the decisions to someone else. It's your life, your money, and your responsibility. Moreover, it's definitely not the time to spend on nonessential items to make yourself feel better for a while in a superficial way.

I have known dozens of widows and divorcees who felt compelled to spend on everything from a new car to a new wardrobe to a long vacation. It made them feel better. It gave them a fresh start of sorts. Try to resist this splurge mentality. You need to hang onto your money right now, not blow it frivolously. There will come a time when you can do something nice for yourself, but that time is not now.

And don't be surprised if you're suddenly asked for a loan by a friend or relative. People figure that if you've come into some money you'll be more than happy to tide them over for a spell. Unless it's a desperate situation, say you're sorry, but no. This money is all you have left to make sure you have a solid financial future.

As things settle down, you might discover you're better off than you feared. Nonetheless, the first few months will be touch-and-go emotionally and financially. You'll probably find that it pays to curtail your spending until your partner's estate is settled, or until your divorce decree is final, and for several months thereafter until you have a good understanding of your flow of funds.

For this exercise, you'll want to start a new notebook with a fresh folder, preferably on your computer for easy access and storage. You can also run these numbers with online calculators. You're about to develop a budget for your present money situation and your future one. It requires you to focus on how you spend your money, make your money, and save your money. It's your financial snapshot, so be as careful as you can when you're itemizing your expenses and income so you can devise an honest budget that will work for you. Budgeting doesn't have to be a painful procedure, but it will take some motivation. Think of it as your blueprint for financial security—one that will allow you to meet your most important goals.

CALCULATING YOUR NET WORTH

Widows will first want to determine the total value of all assets now available to them. Divorced women should already have done this in order to come to an equitable divorce settlement. After you've identified your assets and liabilities, then you can figure out how much you spend and how much you have coming in. Your assets are things of value that you actually own, such as your home, jewelry, a car. Liabilities are obligations to pay, such as loans or credit card debts. Your income consists of your salary or other earnings from freelance or part-time work, plus funds you receive from investments, such as interest on money market accounts, rental income, or dividends from stocks and mutual fund holdings.

This will serve as your balance sheet, or record of your current net worth. By subtracting your total liabilities from your total assets you'll have a rough idea of what you have to work with. Some of your assets are not readily available to you (for example, your home's value), and others represent cash on hand that you can use to pay immediate household expenses. Don't get panicky if your outstanding debts seem overwhelming. Your next step is to create a spending and saving budget that will help you find ways to augment your income and rein in your spending. There are lots of easy online worksheets to help you. Search for net worth calculators on web sites such as Bankrate.com.

For those of you who enjoy pen and paper, you can scribble along here. Or, start a computer document and work

along with me on your laptop. Not every category will apply
to your situation, so skip along to the ones that apply. If you
have started working with a financial planner or advisor, they
may be able to provide this online worksheet for you as well.

YOUR NET WORTH: ASSETS—WHAT YOU OWN

Your annual income: $

Savings account balance: $

Checking account balance: $

Treasury bonds: $

Certificates of deposit: $

Money market accounts: $

Value of your home: $

Value of any other real estate: $

Life insurance payout from your partner's
    employer: $

Other life insurance policies: $

Your partner's pension payout: $

Your pension's value: $

401(k): $

403(b): $

IRA: $

Keogh: $

Cash value of your life insurance: $

Value of any stocks you now own outside of
    your retirement accounts: $

Value of any bonds you now own outside of
    your retirement accounts: $

Value of any mutual funds you now own outside
    of your retirement accounts: $

Other investments: $
Business interests: $
Value of car(s): $
Your furnishings: $
Your clothes: $
Your jewelry: $
Total assets:

YOUR NET WORTH: LIABILITIES—WHAT YOU OWE

Outstanding balance on your house or rental: $
Home equity loans outstanding: $
Credit card balances: $
Car loan or lease payments remaining: $
Education loans outstanding: $
Yearly car insurance payment: $
Health insurance payment: $
Homeowner's or renter's insurance payment: $
Annual property taxes: $
Federal income tax: $
State income tax: $
Local income tax: $
Annual electric bill: $
Annual gas bill: $
Annual phone bill: $
Estimated yearly clothing costs: $
Estimated transportation expenses: $
Annual car upkeep and gasoline expenses: $
Annual tuition expenses for self: $
Annual tuition expenses for children: $
Annual medical bills not covered by insurance: $
Children's clothing expenses: $

Estimated yearly grocery bills: $
Estimated annual travel expenses: $
Other liabilities: $
Total liabilities: $

Net worth = total assets - total liabilities = $

HOW MUCH INCOME DO YOU HAVE?

Let's start with the plus side of your plan. Your mission is to follow the money trail. What money do you have coming in each month? Are there one-time cash injections you expect to invest? In addition to their own income, widows will probably have future income from their partner's estate in the way of Social Security, life insurance payments, employer pension funds, and the like.

Divorcing women might have some form of ongoing spousal support or a monetary division of assets. You might not receive some of these funds for a period of time until things are settled. Make a note of when you can expect to see that cash. Until then, you'll need to rely on your cash reserves or perhaps even borrow funds, which makes watching your spending in these early days extremely important.

Source of Income	Amount of $
Your net income (gross minus taxes)	
Insurance income	
Investment income interest, dividends	
Pension income	
Social Security	

Alimony	
Child support	
Proceeds from sale of home or other real estate	
Other freelance income	
Total income	

HOW MUCH DO YOU SPEND EACH MONTH?

Now you must scrutinize your bills. That means poring over your spending history for the past year. You'll need your credit card statements and checking account records to get a good read on this. Don't forget to include cash expenditures. Expenses that were covered with cash are tough to follow, but do your best to ferret them out.

Divide the bills into categories: housing expenditures (monthly mortgage, rent, and so forth), entertainment, autos, food, utilities, and so on. Then, analyze your findings for ways that you can trim spending. Entertainment expenses, for example, are pretty easy to pare, but utility bills are not so easy to cut.

You can find budget worksheet tools to get control of your spending each month or create yours on websites like Mint. com, Consumer.gov, and Kiplinger.com. Your credit card providers may provide you with year-end statements that you can download to your computer. These statements typically break down your annual spending by categories and can be a big help and time-saver here.

You'll discover that you have two types of monthly expenses. There are fixed expenses that you are obligated to pay each month, no matter what; for example, your mortgage, cell phone or landline bill, or car payment. Then there are those variable expenses that fluctuate month-to-month, such as your electric bill, gasoline costs, and credit card bills.

If you pay your bills online, you will also have an electronic record at your fingertips by logging onto your bank account.

THE CORE BILLS

Core bills are the ones you pay regularly for a set period of time. They might be due annually, monthly, or quarterly, but whatever their interval, they are commitments you made that you are obligated to pay, at least for now. They usually include your mortgage, utility bills, and taxes. Down the road, you'll more than likely be able to cut even these expenses dramatically. Obviously, you won't need two cars anymore if you're a widow—unless you have kids who need wheels, of course. But you may also have new expenses, such as your therapist bills or a personal trainer, a babysitter, or a dog walker if you've been working part-time or are heading back to a full-time job.

You may move to a smaller home that has more affordable upkeep, with a smaller mortgage, slimmer property taxes, and lower water and electric bills. Your grocery bill for one person should definitely be lower than it was for two people, your health insurance payments will be reduced, and so forth. But for now, record what is currently due to help plan your budget for the next few months.

OPTIONAL SPENDING

There are expenses that change each month, and these are the ones you have the most control over immediately. By sorting through the past year's checks and online bank transactions, you're going to get a pretty good picture of where you splurged and where you didn't. Maybe you'll find you shelled out $150 every two months for a haircut and highlighting. Maybe you spent $100 a month on dry cleaning. Other such optional expenses include health club memberships, vacations, magazine subscriptions, movies, and meals out, all of which change frequently and are likely to continue to be variable in the months to come. You can start cutting back on these costs today. Getting a handle on your spending will help you set priorities and allow you to start saving aggressively. The bottom line is that you have to be ruthless about cutting back wherever you can.

Use this framework to track your expenses.

Your Current Expenses —Fixed Outflow				
Expense		Amount $	When due	How often due (monthly, quarterly, annually)
Loans	Car Payment			
	Mortgage			
	Other loans			
Bills	Gas			
	Electric			
	Cell phone			
	Landline			
	Water			
Insurance Premiums	Auto			
	Homeowner			

	Life			
	Health			
	Disability			
Taxes	Federal			
	State			
	Local			
	Self-employment			
	Property			
Co-op/condo fee				
Rent				
TOTAL FIXED EXPENSES				

This will give you an idea of where you can cut back on spending.

YOUR CASH FLOW

To determine your monthly cash flow, subtract your total expenses from your total income. That should give you a rough idea of what you have to work with each month. This is not an exact science, but the exercise should help you get a grip on where you stand today and help you set your future money goals.

The next stage is to track your current spending *daily* for the next two months. To do so, make sure you save all your receipts either electronically or in paper form and make entries daily so you don't inadvertently leave something out. You might want to set some goals for yourself as well. You might, for instance, try to squeeze $20 out of your current expenses to put into a personal fund for yourself. Then, if you are able to save that sum each month, in a few months you can reward yourself with something special just for you, maybe a half day at a spa or a trip to the theater to see a show.

You could also opt for some more serious goal setting. After her partner died, Susan, then thirty-six, decided her goals were to study nursing and to buy a house in five years.

Here are a few rules to keep in mind when setting your goals and planning for your future financial health:

- Your mortgage or rent payments each month should add up to less than 30 percent of your monthly net income.
- Your total debt, excluding your mortgage, should be less than 20 percent of your net income.

Optional Expenses		
Expense	Total for the year	Average per month
Car expenses (gas, repair, and so on)		
Clothing		
Cosmetics		
Computer hardware and software		
Childcare		
Charity		
Bank fees		
Eating out		
Hairdresser		
Drugstore items		
Prescription drugs		
Tuition		

Household help		
Club memberships		
Gifts		
Unreimbursed medical bills		
Vacations		
Public transportation		
Household items (furniture, curtains, and so on)		
Gourmet Groceries		
Alcohol		
Entertaining		
Automatic savings plans (401(k) contribution)		
Movies		
Other entertainment outside the home		
Hobbies		
Legal fees		
Accountant fees		
Credit card finance charges		
Subscriptions to magazines, newspapers		
Books		
Pet care and supplies		
Dry cleaning and laundry		
Misc. expenses		
TOTAL OPTIONAL EXPENSES		

RAMP UP SAVING

Take advantage of your employer's 401(k) or similar retirement plan. Workers under age fifty can contribute up to $18,000 to their employer-provided 401(k) in 2017. Contributions are tax-deductible, and investments grow tax-deferred until withdrawals in retirement.

Invest enough in your 401(k) to qualify for the full match (the amount your employer puts in as a result of your contributions). Most employers require workers to save from 4 percent to 6 percent of pay to get the maximum match. Begin by saving at least 5 percent of your salary and increase the amount by one percentage point every year until you reach 20 percent. Some plans allow participants to schedule automatic increases each year.

Women often put their own needs last, says Cindy Hounsell, founder of WISER. "They often choose to save for a child's education over their own retirement, for example, or work in a family business for no pay."

Women also live longer than men (81.2 years versus 76.4 years), according to statistics from the United States Department of Health & Human Services. "Living longer and needing more money for the extra years for healthcare, medical expenses and long-term care needs, creates serious problems for women," Hounsell says.

Women increasingly worry about running out of money in retirement and managing the rising costs of health insurance, according to "Women, Money and Power," a study from the Allianz Life Insurance Company of North America.

When it comes to saving for healthcare costs in retirement, women need to set aside almost 20 percent more than men, on average, to cover their medical bills in the final years of their lives, according to a report, "The High Cost of Living

Longer: Women & Retirement Health Care," from HealthView Services, a company in Danvers, Massachusetts, that provides retirement healthcare data and tools to financial advisors.

The reason for this gap is simple: longevity. The report found that a healthy sixty-five-year-old woman who retired in 2016 and lives to age eighty-nine will have expected healthcare outlays of more than $300,000 on Medicare premiums and out-of-pocket costs for hearing, dental, and vision care. For men, the projected cost is about $260,000. (These projections do not take into account the cost of medical care for those with annual incomes exceeding $85,000 for singles, who can expect to pay surcharges on premiums for Medicare Parts B and D. The figure also does not include projections for any nursing or long-term care costs.)

Sorry for the bad news. But it is a reality check and why you must get serious about taking control in order to become the money-confident woman you will be.

There are several good software programs and online apps that can help you set up a budget and manage your money. Check out YouNeedABudget.com, Mint.com, LearnVest.com, and the comprehensive Quicken Home and Business (quicken. com). These online personal finance tools can help you track your spending habits, budget, and more.

In the next chapter, you'll learn how to seek professional help to put together a financial plan for the next year, or for five, ten, or more years down the line.

CHAPTER RECAP

In this chapter, we discussed:

□ How to put a budget together
□ Figuring your net worth
□ The importance of saving

CHAPTER FIVE

GETTING FINANCIAL ADVICE

As the novelist Agatha Christie once wrote, "Those who never think of money need a great deal of it." Maybe you are fortunate enough to have enough money to live on comfortably for the rest of your life. But chances are, even if your partner left you with ample assets, you'll still need to prepare yourself to manage those funds so they will always be there for you. Your goal is to protect those assets and make them grow for your future and your children's.

No one is going to look after your money the way you can. It's yours to lose. So you have to make it your responsibility to understand the investment process and make decisions about how you want to invest your money.

You might not think so, but you are ready to manage your own money. It's time to take charge. Over time, it's a skill you can learn and master. It just takes a disciplined approach and an ability to handle some risk.

Now that you've figured out your net worth and established a budget, it's time to put your assets to work. Your goal is to have a nice mix of stocks and bonds that provide a balanced portfolio suitable for your age and future money needs. Certainly, there's a bit of luck involved, but there is nothing mystical or magical about investing successfully. You can develop a financial plan and investment strategy to ensure that you will never lack for money.

Chapter Six will explain the universe of investment opportunities from which you may choose, but for now you will probably want to get some money advisors on your team. In time, you will be confident enough to handle your own affairs quite nicely or at least be at ease having the discussions and mapping out your strategy with your trusted advisor.

THE FIRST YEAR

Go slowly! The first year is tough. You've just lost a partner. Your entire world is shifting. Your secure financial world grounded on the power of two may be going utterly haywire (along with everything else) and you don't know what to deal with first.

After you've negotiated your way through the must-do list and located crucial documents, take five. Even though you'll feel anxious to make major financial decisions, most financial advisors counsel that you resist doing so, as I have told you more than once. It bears repeating. These are edgy times, and you're probably not yet prepared to make knowledgeable and practical decisions. So postpone those actions for six months to a year (preferably a full year), and use the time to get up to speed on personal finances.

You may lose some potential short-term gains, but you're not ready to make a move that might cost you the financial assets you have gained from your partner's estate or divorce settlement. This is one time when playing it safe will serve you well.

You'll have the funds invested (no under-the-mattress plan here) but it will be stashed in liquid bank savings accounts, certificates of deposit, money market accounts, or Treasury bills. (If your deceased partner had a solid working relationship with a financial services firm that you feel is capable, you might just hold steady right where you are, until you' ready to make some decisions to suit your own investment needs.) The core message here is no rash moves shifting things around or making big investment decisions.

I like the idea of sitting chilly in these low-profile investments which will guarantee your principal and pay you, say, a modest amount of interest for a one-year CD. Check out Bankrate.com for a list of institutions with top-yielding CDs and money market accounts.

For the long term, these kinds of investments are far too conservative (we'll get into this in-depth later), but until you can make clearheaded choices, you're better off taking the unadventurous route. I'll say it once again: Whatever you do, ignore any uninvited tips or advice from well-meaning friends and relatives. Nine times out of ten the investments will be completely inappropriate for you.

When you're ready to take action, it is a good idea to set up an appointment with a financial advisor to help you develop a short- and a long-term investment plan. In the first several months of being on your own, your priorities are paying your bills and getting a handle on your financial situation. After six months or so, you should be ready to start taking a closer look at your assets and investments to see if they are going to be able to meet your future financial goals.

Be sure that you set up a master file to keep track of any paperwork generated by your new active role in your financial plans. You can also store this information online, but I personally also save paper copies of bank and brokerage account statements. In the end, planning your financial future is solely your responsibility, but you don't have to do it alone.

SELECTING A FINANCIAL ADVISOR

Putting together a financial plan takes time and plenty of patience. That's why for many women in your situation, it's a smart idea to seek a professional to help you get your plan in motion. There are myriad people out there who bill themselves as financial advisors. These include financial advisors, financial consultants, financial planners, life insurance agents, money managers, and stockbrokers, among many others.

And the array of investment choices is staggering: dozens of bonds, from zero-coupon bonds to government bonds to junk bonds to bunny bonds; thousands of mutual funds and Exchange Traded Funds (ETFs) that invest in everything from real estate to foreign currencies; and, of course, a mind-boggling number of companies that sell shares of their stock on the public exchanges. The sheer scope of investment choices today makes a convincing argument for hiring a reliable advisor who can help you make sense of it all, and possibly remain a team member on your personal board of directors for years to come. But who should you pick for that critical mission, and where will you find the best candidate for the job? Your first move is to make sure you understand the different types of advisors, what they can do for you, and what you will pay for their services.

WHAT YOU NEED TO KNOW ABOUT FINANCIAL PLANNERS

A financial planner will typically charge you something, perhaps up to $1,000, for a basic financial plan. But that might be well worth it should you find someone who offers unbiased advice about the best course of action for your unique situation. It doesn't have to be any more than just a road map, so to speak. It will allow you to create a future financial scenario for yourself. Right now, you just have your current snapshot of what's in place today.

Your planner's job is to take stock of your entire financial universe from the materials you provide, such as your statement of net worth and your monthly budget. Then, based on your stated objectives and goals—you need to pay for a child's college education, you want to go back to graduate school, you want to buy a vacation home, you want to retire in 15 years, and so forth—the planner will help you fashion an overall financial strategy not restricted to investments only.

The plan should cover the gamut from taxes to investments to estate planning issues, and should be fairly comprehensive. Moreover, you should expect it to contain recommendations for specific investments, with their future returns projected. Your planner should also be able to give you advice on your insurance needs, get your estate plan in motion, and connect you with other professionals who can pick up those roles.

I'll discuss more about estate planning and the importance of wills in Chapter Eight. If all goes well, you will have an ongoing relationship with the planner and receive quarterly statements reviewing your financial situation. Then, too, you'll probably meet once or twice a year to make changes and adjustments.

Finding a good financial planner whom you can trust with your finances can be tricky, though. In general, you're better off if you work with a fee-only planner.

Fee-only planners charge an up-front fee for their advice. It can be a percentage of your portfolio (say, 1 percent to 2 percent), a per-hour charge, or a basic fee per planning session. They don't, however, make any commissions from the investments they recommend. To get a list of fee-only planners in your area, visit the websites of the National Association of Personal Financial Advisors, the Financial Planning Association, and the Certified Financial Planner Board of Standards.

Another excellent source of financial advice is the Association for Financial Counseling and Education® (AFCPE.org) website. An Accredited Financial Counselor (AFC) can address your immediate money challenge and help you create a plan to achieve your goals. You can search by location and area of expertise. Fees typically start around $200 an hour, but vary. Virtual sessions are possible.

The key is to feel comfortable with the planner and be assured that he or she has your best interests in mind. The more sophisticated you are about investing, the less handholding you will need. It pays to spend some time meeting and interviewing at least three potential planners. Doing so will give you a better feel for the kind of advice you're likely to get, and you'll sense what kind of person you'll click with.

Some fee-only planners charge an annual retainer or a flat fee. What that flat fee is can range greatly based on your assets and the type of planning you need. An overall strategy with ongoing asset management, for example, would be pricier than a one-time estate planning session.

Other fee-only planners charge hourly rates. Hourly rates average about $100 to $400. Always get a quote of the total hours you'll be billed before you hire a planner who bills by the hour.

Another type of planner is a **fee-plus-commission planner**. These planners typically bill you a set fee and earn commissions on some of the investments they recommend. Then there are

commission-only planners. They are similar to stockbrokers and insurance agents in that they earn a commission on the investments you buy through them. Their employer pays them to sell the product to you. This is not necessarily bad, but it does pose the question of whether there is a conflict of interest. Are they just telling you to buy something so they can land a sweet commission, or is it really a good product for you? If the investment turns out to be a solid performer, it hardly matters if they get paid for their advice that way. But if it goes sour, it could leave you with a bad taste in your mouth.

That's why I recommend that you shop for an advisor who will sign an agreement to act as a fiduciary, which means that he or she agrees to act solely in your best interest when giving advice or recommending investments for your retirement accounts. Not all advisors are fiduciaries as of this writing, so it's up to you to make sure that your financial advisor is looking out for you. Signing an agreement to act as a fiduciary is no assurance of respectable behavior, but it's a way to sort out salespeople who label themselves advisors.

It's important, in my opinion, to seek advisors or planners who have a Certified Financial Planner (CFP) accreditation. A CFP is a professional who has completed a rigorous series of courses and exams in financial planning and undergoes hours of continuing education each year. To access a database of planners, go to cfp.net.

WORKING WITH A FULL-SERVICE INVESTMENT BROKER

A brokerage is, quite simply, an intermediary between buyers and sellers of stocks and other securities. Before you select a stockbroker to execute your financial transactions, you should understand just how he or she expects to be paid for this service and how you can cut those costs. A broker earns his or her income by the commissions paid on investments you buy or sell.

It's sometimes uncomfortable to talk about money and, especially, compensation issues. But don't be timid about asking your broker how he or she is to be paid for a particular investment.

This is not the time for you to be playing around with high-risk investments. While you are beginning to move your funds out of conservative certificates of deposit, you should stick to a somewhat cautious strategy for a while longer and slowly add riskier choices to your mix.

In the meantime, watch out for brokers who recommend frequent transactions. For most of us, buying and holding for at least a three-year time horizon is usually more appropriate. But brokers make money on every trade they make, so they have an incentive to keep it rolling.

Meanwhile, you could be eligible for some discounts on commissions. Some brokers lower commissions on in-house mutual funds if you invest a minimum of $25,000 or so in one fund. Then, too, brokerages will frequently offer discounts to their best customers—in other words, someone with a hefty sum under their management. If you really want to shave commissions, you can trade through a discount brokerage house such as Charles Schwab, Fidelity, or TD Ameritrade.

But don't expect to receive any investment advice or additional services from discount brokerages. When you hire a full-service broker, you receive extra attention. For example, you can request research reports from the brokerage's analysts, as well as other detailed research reports from firms like Morningstar and Bloomberg. Moreover, your broker should be available to meet with you one-on-one at least every four months to go over your investments and take your calls and emails at the drop of a hat.

As with planners, it's smart to ask for recommendations from colleagues and other people you respect. You might also check with women you've met through support groups and the like who have found a broker who understands their special needs. Again, you'll want to interview two or three brokers to see what kinds of investments they would suggest given your situation. You should also do your due diligence. Never be swayed by a broker who cold-calls you at home offering investment tips. Then, too, do your own independent research before handing over any funds.

To look up the public record on registered investment advisors, contact the Securities and Exchange Commission (advisorinfo.sec.gov). BrokerCheck (brokercheck.finra.org) is another place to check on employment history and exams passed, as well as any consumer complaints or whether the broker has been sanctioned.

Here are a few basic items to check:

- Does the advisor's name appear in BrokerCheck? If not, he or she is not licensed. Check under "disclosure events" to find cases where an advisor's behavior may have had complaints. This can include inquiries by state or federal regulators. They may have been proven innocent, so this is not necessarily a black mark. Read the entire entry. While most advisors have spotless records, about 7 percent of brokers registered with FINRA have some transgression on their record.

- It's good to get a bead on how long someone has worked for a firm. If someone job-jumps, he or she may not be the right person for you. Stability is the name of the game for you as you build your money confidence. A BrokerCheck report will list an advisor's employment past.

- It's also a good idea to do a quick internet search on any current or potential advisors to see if anything pops up that reflects poorly on their track record. Some state securities regulators also offer reports that provide a fuller picture of an advisor's record, but the availability of these reports varies widely. PIABA (Public Investors Arbitration Bar Association, piaba.org/) has a list and contact information for the state agencies.

- Tap into the tools offered by the Investor Protection Trust (iinvest.org/tools-resources/) to learn more.

DON'T OVERLOOK INVESTMENT FEES

There is an array of fees that are charged when you buy and sell, or work with an advisor. It's important to be a smart consumer. Investment and brokerage fees cut into your investment returns over the long-haul. If your portfolio was up 8% for the year but you paid 1.5% in fees and expenses, your return is really only 6.5%. Over time, that difference can add up to a big chunk of lost earnings.

You can suss out the nitty-gritty details of what you are paying in fees in various places. A broker's website will have a page devoted to account fees. With your 401(k), check out the summary plan description of the various funds you have invested in, and there will be a clear outline of the specific investments offered by the plan, with fees and expenses. Mutual funds always have a section outliing fees and expenses in their description. Robo-advisors, firms that manage your investments via a computer algorithm, often charge significantly less. That's because there's not a human in the middle making the decisions. A standard fee is 0.25% of assets or less; some advisors offer computer supervising with financial advisor help and will charge a bit more. Management fees will be listed on their websites.

TERMS TO BECOME FAMILIAR WITH

- **Brokerage account fees:** There are annual fees to maintain a brokerage account.
- **Expense ratios:** These are fees charged each year by mutual funds, index funds and exchange-traded funds, as a percentage of your investment.
- **401(k) fees:** These are the underlying management fees of mutual funds offered by your employer.
- **Management or advisory fees:** This is often a percentage of assets under management, paid by you to a financial advisor.
- **Sales loads:** A sales charge or commission on some mutual funds.
- **Trade commissions or transaction fee:** Charged by a financial services firm when you buy or sell certain investments, such as stocks or mutual funds.

Choosing the right money advisor for you takes legwork, and you have to follow your own instincts about the individual. It's a gut feeling. Then, too, a broker or planner who works beautifully with your friend or your Aunt Ann might not have the expertise to handle your situation, or you could have a personality conflict that makes it hard to communicate.

Communication is paramount though. Revealing your most intimate money profile to a stranger takes trust and confidence. It makes you feel vulnerable in some way. Take whatever time you need to find the right individual.

This is a business decision. It's not personal. Your advisor doesn't have to be your confidant, but he or she does have to be someone you can talk to face-to-face and not someone who talks down to you or is condescending in any fashion. After all, you're the customer. You deserve that respect. Remember, you're the employer, hiring someone to work for you—not the other way around.

Having a competent financial advisor can make the transition to financial independence smoother than if you were to attempt to navigate the way completely on your own. It can also save loads of time that might be better spent on other duties. Nonetheless, the key to a successful partnership is going to be your own involvement and understanding of the decisions you are making that will affect you and your family for years to come. Chapter Six will give you a crash course in investing, and you'll begin to get a clearer understanding about the specific kinds of investments you are going to be selecting.

QUESTIONS TO ASK A POTENTIAL INVESTMENT ADVISOR

- How long have you been a planner?
- How many years have you worked for this firm?
- Can you tell me some details about the firm's history and the areas you specialize in?

- What are your qualifications?
- What professional groups do you belong to?
- Do you take part in any continuing education programs? How often?
- What percentage of your clients are women?
- What percentage are divorced?
- What percentage are widowed?
- How big are your client's portfolios on average?
- How are you paid?
- What is your area of strength from an investment perspective?
- What is your money philosophy?
- Are you registered with the Securities and Exchange Commission?
- Can you give me three references?
- What was your worst investment last year?
- What was your best investment in the past 12 months?
- How do your contracts work? Are they written or oral?
- Are there any restrictions on terminating your services?
- What can I expect from you in the way of services?
- How often will we meet?
- Based on what you know about my financial situation and objectives, what types of investments do you think would be appropriate, and over what time horizon?

QUESTIONS A PROFESSIONAL ADVISOR SHOULD ASK YOU

- How old are you?
- How long have you been divorced? Widowed?
- Do you have any dependents?
- What are your assets?
- What are your liabilities?
- What is your total income?
- What are you likely to receive in alimony?
- How much did you receive in insurance payouts from your partner's estate?
- What is the current value of your home?
- Do you rent?
- What are your housing costs each month?
- What are your total expenses each month?
- What are your goals and objectives?
- Do you have a will in place?
- Do you have life insurance?
- What other insurance coverage do you have—health, automobile, homeowner's?
- What is your money philosophy?
- Are you a conservative investor or are you willing to tolerate some risk?
- Are you savvy about investing?
- How much money management can you handle by yourself?
- What will you need a professional to help you with?
- What benefits does your employer provide?
- How much have you saved in retirement accounts?
- Will you inherit money one day?
- Do you expect to remarry in the next year or so?
- Are you planning to go back to school?

CHAPTER RECAP

In this chapter, we discussed:

- ☐ The different kinds of financial advisors
- ☐ How to check up on a broker
- ☐ What questions to ask a potential advisor

CHAPTER SIX

INVESTING 101

If you've followed the advice in this book and put your lump-sum insurance payout or divorce settlement funds in savings accounts, low-paying certificates of deposit, money market accounts, or Treasury bills, and not made any rash moves with other inherited investment accounts, good for you.

You've avoided making any hasty decisions. If you have no investing experience, you'll want to use the next several months to learn about investing, even if you are working with a financial pro.

It's not as hard as you might think. But it's worth as much of your attention as you can spare. Before you start actively handling your money, you need to be sure that you're financially literate.

One good way to start educating yourself is to get into the habit of reading the financial pages of your local newspaper and poring over *The Wall Street Journal*, either at the library or by subscribing for a few months or more. You might even consider subscribing to a personal finance magazine such as *Kiplinger's Personal Finance* or *Money*, which are also available online. Other financial sites, such as Forbes.com and YahooFinance.com, are also good sources. They aim to teach people about investing in a plain, straightforward manner that they can grasp without too much effort. Check out the websites

I've mentioned as well such as CNBC.com's investing section, Learnvest.com, NextAvenue.org's Money & Security section on its site, Nerdwallet.com's blog on investing topics, and Dailyworth.com.

Make money a regular topic of conversation with your most trusted girlfriends. You don't need to plunge right into which stocks or mutual funds you're investing in. Take it slowly.

Begin by asking for tips on a financial topic that you want to know more about. Women love to give advice; you and your friends probably do it all the time, recommending the best local stores, doctors, and restaurants. Once you and your friends get comfortable talking about money, you can then venture into discussions about investing.

Ask about articles they've read and casually mention any you've seen. You might even suggest financial writers to follow on Twitter or "Like" on Facebook. Then, you can chat about what you've gleaned from their postings. The key is to weave money into the fabric of a routine chat.

Start a money book club. Women love book clubs; I'm asked to join them all the time. The good thing about a money book club is that it can force you to read books you might never have picked up on your own.

If possible, invite a local financial author or financial journalist from the local paper (or its website) to stop in for a session. A free meal might be the only lure you need.

Create a money-circle discussion group. A money-circle group lets you and your friends institute regular conversations about finances. You might start the circle discussions by sharing such stories as what each of you was taught about money as a child, your first money experiences, how your parents handled money, and your worst money mistakes. Then, move into conversations about recent money moves you've made, encouraging one another. Above all, make your money klatches positive. And don't let the money discussions devolve into any kind of competition.

In my experience, men consider investing to be a game; often, bragging seems to be the tenor of their money conversations. But it's not about who's smarter or richer. It's about how we'll reach our financial goals together.

Your goal is to familiarize yourself with the various terms. Yes, it's jargon, but it's jargon worth learning. Again, even if you use the services of a financial planner or money manager to help put together an investment plan, that doesn't mean you can afford to remain clueless about your finances.

Educate yourself online. I suggested a few web resources previously on how women can become more confident investors. The National Endowment for Financial Education's Smartaboutmoney.org has free guides that explain stocks, bonds, and mutual funds.

Another site I particularly like for women (that I mentioned earlier) is WISER (wiserwomen.org), which is operated by the nonprofit Women's Institute for a Secure Retirement (WISER). This site has an excellent, straightforward tutorial on the basics called Investment 101, as well as many articles for women looking for more sophisticated investing advice. The group also offers workshops across the country.

You may not want to take on the financial responsibility of learning to invest. Ignore it long enough and it will go away, right? Just hand it all over to cousin So-and-so, who purports to have all the answers and a bag of can't-miss investments for you. Don't. Taking charge of your finances while you are grieving the loss of a partner is not something anyone is eager to do, but you may pay dearly for not doing so.

The kinds of investments that will work best for you will depend on a variety of factors, but the most important will be your age, the amount of money you have available to invest, your debt load, your monthly expenditures, and whether there are others who rely on you to live—perhaps children or elderly parents. There are thousands of ways to invest your money, some far riskier than others, and it's important to know just how much risk (which is a measure of possible loss in value) you can take with your money.

For example, investing in stocks can be dicey over the short term. Yet over every 20-year period since 1931, stocks have outperformed interest-paying investments. In fact, no one can afford not to invest in stocks these days. But unless you're the next Warren Buffett, you might opt for mutual funds to accomplish this goal. Buying and selling individual shares takes nerves of steel and quite a bit of research to know which ones to buy and precisely when to sell.

For the most part, women hate taking on that kind of risk. It's a psychological thing. If an investment flounders, we internalize the loss and blame ourselves, while men are more apt to shrug their shoulders and chalk it up to bad luck or their brokers' mistakes. But making your money work for you is critical. Once you understand what investing is all about, you'll have the confidence to do so.

DIVERSIFY INVESTMENTS

Aim for a portfolio of stocks or stock mutual funds. Equities outperform fixed-income investments over time. Investors more than fifteen years from retirement might consider an aggressive portfolio with more than 80 percent allocated to stocks.

Invest in a diverse mix of low-cost index funds. You might select a trio of funds: a broad United States stock market index fund, an international stock market index fund with exposure to both developed and emerging markets, and an index fund that invests in the overall United States bond market.

Another option: Target-date funds, or TDFs, which automatically adjust the balance of their stock and fixed-income investments based on your age. More on these shortly.

Here are your three key investment objectives: growth, income, and safety. In general, safety isn't always the best route to take, but there are times in your life when it is the wisest way to go. For instance, you should opt for safety during those first few months after you've started managing your money solo, as discussed previously. As time goes on, you can gradually move into more aggressive, higher-growth investments. It's important to have the right mix of stocks, bonds, and cash and to maintain a balanced portfolio that lets your money grow without risking principal.

Before you make any investment, make sure you understand how liquid that investment is. **Liquidity** is a measure of how quickly you can retrieve your funds. You'll also want to know how safe the investment is. What is the likelihood that you won't get your money back at all? And finally, you'll want to know what the investment's rate of return is likely to be, or what it will earn. In general, safe investments have the lowest returns and may not even beat inflation in some years.

One rule many financial advisors suggest: the percentage of your portfolio invested in stocks or stock mutual funds should be one hundred and fifteen minus your age. The remainder should be divided between bonds and bond mutual funds. When you're in your thirties, you'll aim for long- or intermediate-term bonds. As you grow older, you will shift to fixed-income bonds and then into CDs and money market accounts or funds.

Here are the major investment categories to consider:

Money Market Accounts

These accounts are offered by financial institutions around the country and may require a minimum deposit of up to $2,500. They typically pay a slightly higher, variable interest rate than a plain-vanilla savings account, and importantly, they are liquid. The account is federally insured. Nonetheless, when you take into consideration taxes and inflation, these accounts are usually a poor choice for any significant amount of your portfolio over any lengthy period of time.

Fixed-income Investments

Simply put, a fixed-income investment is one that pays you a certain rate of return over a specific time frame. Here are the most common fixed-income investments.

Certificates of Deposit (CDS)

A certificate of deposit is a product usually sold by a bank or brokerage house that pays a fixed rate over a fixed term. The time period usually runs from three months to five years. And you are generally required to invest a minimum amount, anywhere from $500 to $2,500. If you have invested through a federally insured institution, the federal government guarantees up to $250,000 through the Federal Deposit Insurance Corporation (FDIC), thus making CDs a very secure investment. If you withdraw your money before the term is over, however, you'll be hit with an early-withdrawal penalty that in the early stages can gobble up part of your principal. Drawback: The rates CDs pay can be low.

It's important to do your homework before locking yourself into a CD term. Bankrate.com runs charts listing the best rates in the country.

Bonds

When it comes to fixed-income investments, most people think of bonds, and there are many varieties of them. To put it in the simplest terms, when you buy a bond, you're making a loan to the issuer—the federal government or a corporation. The issuer agrees to pay you a set rate of income, known as the coupon rate. That interest is typically paid to you on a quarterly schedule. At the end of the term, the bond matures and you are repaid in full for the principal amount you originally loaned. The key is to hold onto the bonds until maturity (the date at which the bond is payable).

Bonds provide the ballast to hold things steady when the stock market slips and slides. No, they don't offer the potential upside that stocks generally do. But bonds do provide a fixed return that repays you the original amount you invested plus interest.

To put it simply, when you buy a bond—whether it's a taxable version from either the federal government or a corporation or a tax-free municipal bond—you're making a loan to the issuer. Municipal bonds and muni bond funds may be attractive for higher-income investors, since their interest is free from federal taxes. If the bonds are issued by your state, they may be free from state and local taxes too.

Bond values fluctuate primarily depending on interest rates and the financial health of the issuer. The general rule is that when interest rates go up, bond prices go down and vice versa.

Bond rating services, like Moody's (Moodys.com) and Standard & Poor's (standardandpoors.com), appraise the security of those investments; the safest are in the AAA category. Typically, the highest-rated, most secure bonds are issued by the U.S. government and its agencies.

How much of your portfolio should be in bonds? It's impossible to generalize, but my financial advisor suggests that since I'm in my mid-fifties, I should currently hold about 65 percent of my retirement portfolio in stocks and 35 percent in bonds. And I do.

Money pros typically say that as you get older you ought to increase bond holdings and reduce your exposure to the stock market. That's because you'll have fewer years to compensate for any downturn in the stock market and, without a full-time income in retirement, you'll be counting on your investments to help cover your living expenses.

GETTING STARTED INVESTING IN BONDS

Invest in bond mutual funds or bond ETFs. Most women I know own bonds primarily through bond mutual funds (which hold an assortment of bonds) and exchange-traded bond mutual funds, or ETFs, which are similar. That's what I do.

With bond funds and bond ETFs, fees and minimum investments tend to be low. You can often buy a bond fund for $3,000; ETFs trade like stocks, so there's no fixed minimum investment. The best part about bond funds and bond ETFs is that they make it very easy to diversify, particularly if you opt for a total bond index fund, such as the Vanguard Total Bond Market Index Fund (ticker symbol: VBMFX). It invests about 70 percent in U.S. government bonds and 30 percent in corporate bonds. Vanguard has a similar ETF: Vanguard Total Bond Market ETF (BND).

If you'd rather buy a bond fund or ETF that's actively managed—whose skipper decides which bonds to buy and sell—you might consider the PIMCO Real Return Fund (PRRIX) or its ETF cousin, PIMCO Total Return Fund (PTTRX). Both invest primarily in high-quality taxable bonds.

Or buy individual bonds and "ladder" them. With laddering, you buy a few bonds from the same issuer and each one has a somewhat longer maturity date than the next. For example, you could invest $50,000 by purchasing five $10,000 bonds with terms ranging from one to five years.

With individual bonds, you won't lose money if bond prices drop as long as you hold the securities until maturity. But bond funds are forced to sell when they have redemptions, so they may need to sell holdings at a loss. The purpose of laddering is that you'll sell the bonds at different times, when you might need the money, rather than waiting for them all to come due at once.

Consider Treasury Inflation-Protected Securities (TIPS). TIPS aim to shield investors from inflation because the returns of these U.S. Treasury bonds are tied to the Consumer Price Index. To learn more, go to treasurydirect.gov.

Here's how TIPS work: If you buy $10,000 in TIPS and the annual inflation rate is 3 percent, your principal will be worth $10,300 by the end of a year. TIPS pay interest every six months, which is exempt from state and local taxes but subject to federal taxes.

My last piece of advice, no matter which bonds you consider: Consult a financial advisor. A professional can help match your portfolio to your life stage, risk tolerance, and amount you can afford to invest.

Becoming a Bonds Girl might not be the sexiest way to invest, but it could produce blockbuster results for your portfolio. There are three main types of bonds you can buy. These are government bonds, municipal bonds, and corporate bonds.

Government Bonds

U.S. savings bonds are thought to be the safest bond investments because they are backed by the U.S. government. Moreover, the interest is tax-free. For widows, these bonds are usually a good investment because they offer a steady income stream. There are three different kinds of government bonds. **Treasury bills** mature in terms of sixty days to one year. **Treasury notes** have terms of one to ten years. **Treasury bonds** mature in anywhere from ten to thirty years. Of course, the shorter the term, the lower your interest rate will be.

You can buy these government bonds through a broker, but the U.S. Treasury Department does have a program called Treasury Direct that sells the bonds without a service fee (treasurydirect.gov) or from a regional Federal Reserve Bank. And you can now have the Treasury deduct the amount you wish to invest directly from your bank account (previously, standard procedure required you to send a certified check or cashier's check). Moreover, you can reinvest the funds from your maturing bonds twenty-four hours a day, three hundred and sixty-five days a year by phone instead of mail.

Municipal Bonds

Municipal bonds (munis) are issued by city, local, or state governments. Again, any interest paid by the bonds is free from federal taxes and, if issued by the state in which you live, is additionally spared from state and local taxes. There are two types of municipal bonds: general obligation and revenue. If the bond is backed by the issuing city or state, it is called **general obligation**. If it is backed by a specific project (for example, a toll road), then it is considered to be **revenue**.

You should always look for muni bonds that are rated at least A or higher by the rating agencies. You can invest in munis that are guaranteed to repay your principal and any interest earned.

Corporate Bonds

Corporate bonds are issued by a corporation. Again, look for the highest ratings possible to shield your investment. Remember, though, the lower-rated bonds will generally pay a higher interest rate. The more risk you take, the more you stand to earn. Your earnings on corporate bonds, paid twice a year, are fully taxable. For the most part, these bonds are purchased in multiples of $1,000.

Corporate bonds with the lowest ratings are called **junk bonds**. They often have no rating assigned to them at all. The risk here is that the corporation may go belly-up and you are out your entire investment. Chances are you'll want to steer clear of junk bonds completely.

WHAT YOU NEED TO KNOW ABOUT STOCKS

It's true that stocks are far riskier than any of the investments we've discussed so far in this chapter. But you can't ignore the upside potential. Risky or not, you must learn to live with them. Put plainly, over the long run, stocks generally outperform fixed-income investments like bonds. Over short time frames they can zig and zag like a roller coaster ride. When you invest in stocks, you should always do so for a time frame of at least three to five years.

Moreover, if you continue to hold a stock investment over time, you reap the benefits of compounding, a combination of your principal investment and subsequent dividends and interest, that keep it growing. Stocks offer you the possibility for growth that everyone needs in order to be financially secure in the future.

What exactly are stocks? They are shares in a corporation that are sold to generate money for the firm. Common stock generally has greater potential for appreciating in value than does preferred stock. Currently, there are roughly six thousand companies trading shares on the big exchanges—the New York Stock Exchange and the National Association of Securities Dealers Automatic Quotation system (NASDAQ). One method of tracking the overall health of the stock market is major market indicators: S&P 500 and Dow Jones Industrial Average. The Dow Jones Industrial Average is a price-weighted average of thirty significant stocks traded on the New York Stock Exchange and the Nasdaq, including GE, Disney, and Apple.

Hundreds of millions of shares are traded daily, and picking the cream of the crop can be difficult at best. When you buy shares from a major brokerage you will usually be charged a commission. Discount brokerages will lower that commission, but you shouldn't expect much in the way of service or investment advice for that.

For the more confident do-it-yourself investors, there are about four hundred public companies that allow you to buy shares directly from them without going through a broker at all. You will pay some fees, but in general they are far less imposing. You may also have to make a minimum investment. Some of the companies offering these direct stock purchase plans include Walmart, Ford Motor Company, and Tiffany & Co. If you're buying a very small number of shares and want to minimize your costs, a direct stock purchase is a great way to go.

To get a list of companies that let you buy directly from them, go to DRIPCentral.com for a minimum investment of between $50 and $1,000 or more. You might even consider joining or starting an investment club, a group of people who research stocks and pool their money together to invest as one entity. The National Association of Investment Companies (naicpe.com) can help you get started.

BASIC TYPES OF STOCKS

Blue chip stocks are probably the most familiar. These are typically stocks of well-established corporations like AT&T and General Motors. They are considered to be the best-quality investments and will normally pay dividends, a payout to shareholders based on profits.

Income stocks will pay even higher dividends to investors.

Value stocks are generally undervalued companies which trade at a price below where it appears it should be based on its financial standing. It may have high dividend payout ratios or low financial ratios, such as price-to-book or price-to-earnings ratios.

The **price-to-book** ratio (P/B Ratio) is a ratio used to compare a stock's market value to its book value. It's computed by dividing the current closing price of the stock by the latest quarter's book value per share. The **book value** is a company's assets minus its liabilities. The **price-to-earnings ratio** (P/E ratio) is the ratio for valuing a corporation that measures its current share price in relation to its per-share earnings. The price-earnings ratio is also sometimes identified as the price multiple or the earnings multiple. Keep in mind that a stock price may also have dropped due to public perception regarding factors that have little to do with the company's current operations.

Growth stocks are those shares of companies that have substantial potential for growth in the foreseeable future. Growth companies may currently be growing at a faster rate than the overall markets, and they often invest most of their current revenue toward further expansion. Every sector of the market has growth companies, but they are more common in the arenas of technology, alternative energy and biotechnology.

In each of these categories, you can find small-company stocks are usually the fast growers, but they do carry more risk. International stocks are also a great way to diversify your portfolio, and you can slice and dice by the broad categories listed above. But the risk is compounded by the exchange rate. Hundreds of foreign firms trade in the U.S. in the form of American Depository Receipts, or ADRs.

MUTUAL FUNDS

Stocks are an essential part of a healthy portfolio, so invest boldly. That said, I personally am nervous when it comes to buying individual stocks. For me, and I suspect for most of you, mutual funds are the way to go.

A mutual fund is a selection of bonds and/or stocks that are invested as a pool. They aren't federally insured, but the great thing about mutual funds is that they allow you to diversify your investments, and they are generally managed by professionals. The total pool of securities is divided into shares and sold to investors like us. There are now more than eight thousand mutual funds to choose from, and believe me, it's confusing.

In most cases, the minimum investment is around $500 to $3,000, but you can get into some for less. Once you're in, you can routinely reinvest small amounts on a regular basis. As with stocks, mutual fund share prices, otherwise known as net asset value, rise and fall on a daily basis. But since you are investing in a variety of securities, as opposed to having all your money caught up in one individual company, you have a bit more protection from market swings.

As with stocks, there is a wide range of fund groups, each with a different investment objective—safety, growth, or income. The Financial Industry Regulatory Authority, Inc. (FINRA) has a tool to compare different mutual funds and associated costs. The Fund Analyzer offers information and analysis on over 18,000 mutual funds, Exchange Traded Funds (ETFs) and Exchange Traded Notes (ETNs). This tool estimates the value of the funds and impact of fees and expenses on your investment and allows you to look up applicable fees and available discounts for funds. Go to apps. finra.org/fundanalyzer/1/fa.aspx.

Here are the basic categories of mutual funds.

- **Growth mutual funds** offer a bit more security than small-company funds, but they, too, are unlikely to pay any income and are best held for a longer time horizon, say, five to seven years.
- **Income funds** invest in income stocks such as utilities. You'll receive dividends with these.
- **Growth and income funds** offer a mixture of growth stocks and income stocks. These, too, are for the longer haul.
- **Index funds** mirror indexes like the S&P 500. These are my personal favorites because they offer the lowest fees, since they are not managed by an individual human, but rather a computer's set basket of securities, and have the typically have the least amount of volatility.
- **International funds** are a great way to diversify your investments in the global economy.
- **Sector funds** invest in just one type of industry (for example, technology companies). Some invest in cyclical stocks, such as automakers and homebuilders, whose profitability depends on the strength of the economy.
- **Bond funds** invest in government bonds, international bonds, and the like.
- **Socially conscious funds** invest only in corporations with solid environmental records and so forth. Think no guns or tobacco.

The type of fund or mix of funds that you should be considering now will depend in large part on your needs. Do you need current income in order to live? Can you afford to set aside a chunk for the future (riskier types of funds that will have a chance to grow for you)? The point here is that you have to define your objectives. You have already done some preliminary work on this as you clarified your money profile and drew up your budget. One of the best ways to evaluate a given fund is by its performance record.

Buying mutual funds is not difficult. You can either purchase them through a broker or invest directly in the fund itself. Most funds, such as Fidelity, T. Rowe Price and Vanguard, have a website that gives you the lowdown on the fund's past record and investment objectives. You can fill out the application online in around ten minutes. You will need your Social Security number and a bank account routing number to electronically zap your investment from your bank account, or you can mail a print version along with a check. You can also download the fund's prospectus from the website to learn the nitty-gritty about your investment.

There are thousands of funds today that charge no sales commissions or upfront fees. These are called **no-load funds**, such as the ones I mentioned, and are generally the funds you are going to want to buy. (These are the only ones I buy.) **Load funds**, on the other hand, charge sales fees. Typically, funds bought through a bank or broker are load funds, although increasingly, both banks and brokerages are offering no-load funds as well.

ASSET ALLOCATION

Getting a read on the types of investment choices open to you is a first step toward achieving your goals. However, the key to your success as an investor is knowing how to balance your portfolio in a manner that lets you grow your money over various time periods and protect your principal. This is called asset allocation, and every woman's investment mix will be different.

Your investment mix will depend on your age, in large measure. If you are in your forties and can afford the risk, you might want to have a third of your portfolio invested in large-company stock funds, a quarter in small-company funds, another 15 percent in foreign funds, 20 percent in bonds or bond funds, and a small amount in CDs or money market funds. As you grow older, your balance should shift into less-risky investments like municipal bonds. Diversification, or spreading assets across different types of investments, will help to mitigate your risk.

Another great way to learn to invest regularly is to consider **dollar cost averaging**. This means that you set aside a specific amount of money from your monthly budget, maybe $200, and arrange to have it automatically invested in a particular mutual fund or public stock. That way, you don't have to fret about whether you have timed your investment exactly right. Some months you'll buy high, other months low, and it will all balance out in the end.

Of course, there are many other ways you could invest your money. Collectibles such as artworks or coin collections fit into this category. There are real estate investments you can make aside from your primary home. Although some of these can be wonderfully fun to own and may appreciate over time, they really aren't right for women who are just out on their own in the investing world. Maybe down the road you will be ready to take more chances and have the time to do your homework on some of these opportunities. For now, I'd stick with the basic, straightforward investments that have produced solid returns over time. Keep it simple.

If you already have an investment plan in place and are currently working, here are my eight suggestions for reviewing what you have:

Rebalance your retirement account. This once-a-year technique generally keeps your portfolio from becoming far more aggressive or conservative than you envisioned. Rebalancing means you review your retirement account's stocks versus bonds tilt, see if it matches what you want, and move money around if it doesn't. Financial advisors generally suggest rebalancing whenever your portfolio gets more than 10 to 15 percent away from your original asset allocation.

Workplace 401(k) and similar retirement savings plans increasingly allow you to set parameters for automatic rebalancing. Otherwise, consider using a robo-advisor—an online money manager, such as Wealthfront or Betterment.

Scrutinize how your entire portfolio is divvied up among stocks, bonds, and cash investments. This simple asset allocation is the core of your investments' potential payback, and, of course, risk. It's important to balance your need for the potential upside of future returns with your tolerance for risk.

Portfolios with a greater percentage of stocks have more risk and therefore have a greater fluctuation in value over the short term. But as I have said, they also provide a higher return over time. Over the long run, U.S. stocks have produced gains of close to 7 percentage points a year above inflation. That said, it's probably more realistic today to expect stocks to return around 4 points a year above inflation.

Consolidate your accounts. It's hard enough to get a grip on your investments, but if you have a slew of different statements arriving periodically that you probably don't open, it's even more of a nuisance. Check to see whether you have more than one fund with the same investment objective. If you do, merge them. This is a step you will get to in a few months, but do put it on your to-do schedule.

Consider investing in a target-date fund. To simplify your investments, go with the set-it-and-forget-it strategy. A target-date fund can be a smart way to save for retirement if you don't want to choose and monitor your investments; many people use them for their 401(k)s. A target-date fund automatically adjusts the balance of your fixed-income (bond) investments and stocks based on your age.

Select your target-date fund based on the year you expect to retire. The biggest target-date fund families are Fidelity, T. Rowe Price, and Vanguard, although most financial institutions offer them too.

Roll over any old 401(k) accounts. This is smart housecleaning if you've had several jobs over your career, because inevitably you have retirement money sitting in different accounts. You may also have your deceased partner's account you have inherited and will want to roll over to an IRA.

If you have multiple old 401(k)s of your own, for example, it makes sense to consolidate them into one self-directed rollover IRA through a major mutual fund company.

Shed investments with excessive costs. Check the annual expenses for all your mutual funds. You can find this information easily on the fund company's website page for the fund. If any charge more than 1 percent of assets per year, seek lower-cost replacements—and consider index funds, as I do.

If you're invested primarily in actively managed mutual funds, costs should be a key consideration and reviewed annually. For example, if an actively managed U.S. large-cap fund charges a management fee of 1 percent or more, it pays to switch to an S&P index fund with lower costs. The Vanguard S&P 500 Index Fund, for example, has an annual expense ratio of 0.17 percent.

Weed your stock holdings. Many people own a few stocks in their portfolio that they bought years ago because they either liked the product the company sold or someone recommended it. But they long ago ceased paying attention, or following, the companies' progress and financials. It takes a lot of time to follow individual stocks and to be aware of all the different risks that companies face. This money could be put to better use in a mutual fund or ETF, which provides more diversification.

And don't be afraid to take a loss while you're weeding and sell investments that are not up to snuff. Not all investments work out. The silver lining is that capital losses are tax-deductible. You can take the money you receive from the sale and reinvest it in something with a brighter future.

Finally, consider hiring a financial advisor. Yep. I said it again. I meet annually face-to-face with my financial advisor for have-a-look-under-the-hood summit. We converse throughout the year via emails and a rare phone call.

I grill her on how my investments are doing, tweak my asset allocation to conform to my conservative growth strategy, and discuss where I might redeploy, or add, funds.

You might also consider **gender-based investing**, something that has sparked my interest. Women's workplace issues matter deeply to me and I am always looking for companies to invest in that are making a difference. It's called impact investing.

The overarching concept of gender-based investing is that by finding, and putting money into, companies that support women, you can have a financial and a social impact. You can play a role in helping women gain access to capital to start businesses, fostering workplace pay equity, and supporting firms making products and offering services that advance the lives of women and girls.

As my advisor and I pored over my portfolio (mostly index funds), this year, I realized there wasn't a whole lot of wiggle room to directly apply my lofty values. But we both agreed that gender-based investing was a compelling topic and certainly one that's been gaining traction. The aim is to find public firms with women on their boards, a female founder, women in key decision-making roles, or products and services that promote women's health and well-being.

You might consider investing in one of the firms in the Bloomberg Financial Services Gender-Equality Index (BFGEI). The index includes more than 50 public companies that are leaders in the financial industry for providing opportunities for women. It lists fifty-three data points for each company, ranging from the number of women in the business and on its board to its length of parental leaves. Companies that made the cut include American Express, Bank of America, Barclays, MasterCard, MetLife, and Visa.

State Street Global Advisors offers an ETF (The SPDR® SSGA Gender Diversity Index ETF) that currently invests in 185 companies with notable numbers of women in senior leadership positions. And there's the Pax Ellevate Global Women's Index Fund (paxellevate.com). Sallie Krawcheck, former president of the Global Wealth and Investment Management division of Bank of America, teamed up with fund management company Pax World Management to offer this index fund of companies where women make up a large percentage of officers and directors. Her Ellevate Network firm (ellevatenetwork.com) also has a robo-advisor service for women called Ellevest (ellevest.com), a digital investment platform.

In the next chapter, you'll learn what to do if you and your partner were involved in a family business.

CHAPTER RECAP

In this chapter, we have learned:

☐ How much you know about different investment vehicles

☐ The investing basics you should understand before choosing where to put your money

☐ What to review if your investment plan is already in place

CHAPTER SEVEN

WHEN A BUSINESS IS INVOLVED

It's estimated that more than three million couples operate businesses together. These run the gamut from small law firms to antique stores to consulting practices to fast-food franchises. Both for widows and divorcing women, knowing how to handle your financial affairs when a business is involved is essential. The reason: Your partner's business or your business could be your most valuable asset, far beyond what your home is worth.

GETTING YOUR SHARE

Regardless of the type of business, a mom-and-pop bike shop or deli, it's essential to know just what that business is worth today and what its future growth is likely to be. You'll also want to be aware of any liabilities or debts the firm may have that you would be responsible for paying back. You must get a handle on these figures as soon as you can bring yourself to focus on the larger financial picture.

Any woman who isn't informed about the inner workings of the family company is setting herself up to be taken advantage of either by her ex-partner, her deceased partner's partners, or other foragers. A woman who is naive in matters of business is a conspicuous target for a variety of folks looking to help themselves to the spoils.

For many suddenly single women, a house, an investment portfolio, and maybe jewelry or collectibles come to mind when you think of assets you own, but business interests are not to be overlooked—they can be quite substantial. Sure, there may be other people involved (partners, investors, and the like), but this is one asset you can't afford to ignore. In fact, because of the very nature of its ongoing operation, quickly taking stock is imperative.

If you're going through a divorce, you must have an accurate value of any business interests before your divorce negotiations begin to ensure that you receive an equitable buyout. Take the time to do this.

Separating your personal finances from your partner's is difficult and tension-filled, and so is disentangling yourself from his or her business or your joint company. It's also possible that the roles may be reversed and he or she may be going after a piece of your business. Knowing precisely what that asset is worth ahead of time can help you avoid major financial losses. Ignorance can have a walloping negative impact on your bank account. And that's money you will no doubt need to ease the transition into the next stage of your life.

If your partner is terminally ill, try to get up to speed regarding the business while he or she is still alive and lucid. Discuss where important papers are located and what they think you should do to make it a smooth transition. You need to think hard about your possible future role in the firm. If you're not interested in keeping the company, you'll need to understand your options so you can make wise decisions expeditiously to maximize your asset's value and your future net worth.

Making your way through the financial makeup of the business may seem like a monumental task. Certainly, it's a far tougher assignment than getting your personal papers in order. Nonetheless, a business doesn't stop just because your partner has passed away or you two are splitting up. There are clients to deal with, orders to fill, bills and employees to pay, and much more. It's very possible that you will be called upon in the early days after your partner's death or departure from your life to make major decisions about the future of the firm as it relates to your own best interests. The employees and other managers are in a state of confusion, as well. No doubt they are worried about the future of the company and their jobs.

DETERMINING THE VALUE OF YOUR BUSINESS

You have calculated your net worth and added up your total assets in order to figure out how much money you have on hand. This pool of money is what you have at your disposal to support yourself and family in the days to come. If you are one of those couples who were in business together, or even if one or both of you had your own independent businesses (that is, you didn't work for someone else), the company or companies can represent an enormous amount of money to you.

You may have made a guesstimate about what it all was worth, but now it's time to run the real numbers. Whatever the nature of the business, you'll need to have its value appraised by an unbiased professional. This asset is too important to be appraised by a novice or to try to do it yourself. It's not a guessing matter. It's your future financial health.

Don't panic. You won't have to do the math all by yourself. A forensic accountant can come in handy. A forensic accountant is trained to scrutinize personal and business financial records with an eye not only for what they show, but for what is missing. Most accounting firms have someone with this expertise on staff. There are also professionals who do these kinds of business appraisals for a living. And it's worth paying them for their expertise. I'll tell you how to track down a reputable appraiser. Just be sure you are comfortable with the person you hire and trust that individual. Again, these are apt to be very private, personal financial disclosures.

In a privately held family business, it's not always simple to follow the money trail. There may be outstanding loans that have been done on a handshake alone. The books may not be as neat and up-to-date as they would be for a public company. Needy relatives may be listed as employees even though they don't actually perform much on-site work.

If you are a widow, you may very well want to sell the business, particularly if you weren't active in its day-to-day affairs. That will present a whole set of separate issues for you. Knowing what the business is worth, finding a buyer, and negotiating a successful deal will take time and plenty of clear thinking. Having a professional help you will make the process bearable and, hopefully, make it a profitable venture for you as well.

There may be partners involved who would be interested in buying you out. Then again, you might simply want to throw yourself into the business and learn the ropes or, if you have already been working with your partner, decide to take on more and more responsibilities. Either way, you'll need to get the business assets tallied up in order to put together your financial picture, business plan, and investment strategy.

Beyond the money issues involved, there are legal issues that have to be addressed. You have to be hard-nosed about determining the course of action that will best serve your interests.

If you are divorcing and trying to track down the value of your partner's company, be skeptical of anything he or she passes off to you as "proven documentation" about the financial workings of the firm. There are dozens of wily ways your ex might disguise the company's true value to avoid paying you your fair share. Even if things are amicable on the surface, he or she has a very personal agenda: to hang onto the business and maximize their advantage.

Consider this email Jennifer's husband sent her when she asked for financial information about a firm they co-owned, but she was not active in managing, during their divorce process.

"Jennifer, I sent the information regarding the firm to your accountants–about 35 files. They have a lot of information and ALL are audited financials. I guess your accountants are asking for business information in order to assess the value of the firm. This effort will be very costly, and I believe will not serve any purpose. Not sure what you are trying to do. I guess you are trying make sure that I don't have loans that I didn't disclose or deferred compensation or options or contracts or shareholder agreements or anything that I didn't disclose to you. I don't see how this is useful use of our money."

Hmm. Bingo. He is correct about her accountants, and her concern. All she said to me, when she shared his note, was, "You see what I am dealing with here."

GETTING AN APPRAISAL

You'll definitely want to hire a professional, usually an accountant, who can plow through the company's books and records to determine the value of the computers and other equipment, the building (if it is owned by the company and not a lease situation), and any additional real estate holdings that might be involved. The appraiser will need to know how much income is generated each year and how that is likely to grow over the next several years. There are also intangibles to take into consideration. (For example, how recognizable is the firm's name, and what does this add to its total market worth?)

For widows, don't be duped into accepting your new business partners' or partner's financial rundown of the firm. I know you probably trust these guys and want to leave it to them to keep things going until you have your feet on the ground. Don't. If possible, get an independent evaluation before you even have that first meeting. This will empower you to make wise choices about the dispensation of the company and the role you want to play.

Of course, in the process of divorcing, you can save yourself some money by agreeing to use the same appraiser as your partner—but I'd advise against it. This is one rather large asset for which you should have your own independent appraisal. Even though your partner might be utterly helpful and willing to disclose all on the surface, take a second look.

Certainly, in a down-and-dirty divorce it is not unusual for a partner to try to find ways to disguise a business's true value. He or she might hide profits or pump up the company's expense statements or even list false employees on the roster. There are a million tricks someone can pull to bury a firm's value, so make sure you hire someone who can do some sleuthing for you as well. Nothing is as it appears on the surface—that's a given.

To have a business appraised, you might be able to find someone trustworthy through your attorney or current accountant. Another option is to go to the American Society of Appraisers online (appraisers.org/find-an-appraiser).

Figuring out how to divide up the business will depend in large measure on whether the business is in your name, your ex-partner's name, or owned jointly, as well as the state you live in. In most divorce situations, whoever owns the business will not actually sell it, but rather, will substitute another asset (perhaps your house) for the value you are owed.

That's what Claire did, for instance, in order to make sure she held onto her successful landscaping business. Her partner got the house, as you may recall from the introduction. Then her business fell apart. Though unfortunate, she nonetheless thought she had done the right thing by giving him the house rather than a slice of her business. In some cases, though, you might both agree to sell the business outright, split the funds, and move on.

DIVIDING THE SPOILS

Once you know what the business is worth, then you have to figure out how you are going to proceed: whether to sell it, keep it, or in the case of divorce, possibly split it up. The complexity can be astounding, so make sure you have some reliable people on your team to help figure this out. In addition to the appraiser, these helpers might include an accountant and an attorney.

A business is fully regarded as marital property, similar to your home and other investments. If you are living in a community-property state such as Arizona or California, you will be awarded half of all the assets the two of you accumulated during the marriage. If your partner started the company before you were married, it will be a little tougher to determine just how much is owed to you. The same thing goes if you started your firm before you married him or her. If you began your own business during the marriage, he or she will have rights to it as well.

In the forty-one equitable-distribution states, the business is considered by the courts to be marital property, but don't dream that you are necessarily about to be awarded a full 50 percent of its worth. Equitable distribution may result in a 50/50 split of marital property, or it may skew in favor to one person who raises the children, has less earnings prospects, has given up income chances for the spouse, and so forth.

Typically, once a divorce is filed, you'll have a period of time to file a statement of worth and list all the assets. Don't just blindly trust what your ex's lawyer says the business is worth. The judge will consider a dozen or more other factors before he/she divides the pie. For example, the amount of time and effort you have put into running and growing the business is an important consideration. The more involved you have been, the more payback you will likely receive. In some states, you can even petition to recoup any education expenses you paid for your ex, such as law school tuition.

Try to get your hands on as much information as you can about the company and all its records. If you can get copies of the tax returns for the last five years or so, that's terrific. Knowledge is money, after all. And if you have been a tidy record keeper, you're probably going to be in good shape. You will need hard-copy proof of any money you put into expanding the firm, so go through your files for canceled checks and other documentation. Finally, if you have any joint accounts, or if both of your names are listed on loan documents, you'll want to write to the applicable institutions and tell them to make no transactions without your approval.

NEGOTIATING THE DEAL

Where a business is involved, your current and future tax situation and financial needs will determine how you make a deal. If other partners are involved, it will complicate things further and require some different financial footwork. If you are a widow, you'll want to meet as soon as possible with your partner's partners to set in motion a course that will allow you access to the firm's records. You and the partners should come to a consensus about how you want (and need) to proceed. Make sure you have your lawyer, accountant, or appraiser on hand when you do so. This is a trying time for everyone, and you want to be sure you have a representative who can make sense of it all for you and ask the right questions if you feel unprepared.

In a firm with several partners, there is usually a prior pact, known as a cross purchase agreement, stating that if a partner leaves the firm or dies, the other partners will buy him or her out. In the case of a divorce, the other partners might opt to buy you out or loan your partner money to do so. Partnerships also might have agreed legally when the firm was formed to value the business based on something concrete, like the prior year's profits. A judge might insist on the present-day value, but you can't be sure of that.

Privately owned companies may be tricky enough to figure out, but if the company is public, the process of recouping what you are owed can be even tougher. If you have founder's stock, you'll have to abide by the Securities and Exchange Commission regulations. There could be a six-month waiting period before you can cash out your shares, or you may have to make some public disclosure of your intention to do so well in advance of your actions. Most judges, however, will value your shares at the time you sell, not at the time of the buyout agreement.

WHAT ABOUT TAXES?

Taxes may reduce the amount you receive (what a surprise). If stock shares are involved, there is a very real possibility that you will have to pay capital gains tax when the shares are sold. That will happen if the shares have appreciated in value since you first received them.

If stock is not involved, you'll be fine, because you won't be taxed on a straight transfer of cash—providing your partner pays you off within the time frame imposed by the Internal Revenue Service.

If you do find yourself in the position of having to accept a promissory note from your partner because he doesn't have the resources to pay you off immediately, try to keep the time frame as tight as you can. Also, make sure he or she has something of value to back up that loan—and not your primary home, thank you. The promissory note needs to include some collateral that will default to you if he or she can't pay in the agreed-upon time frame.

CHAPTER RECAP

In this chapter, we have learned:

☐ Why you should hire a forensic accountant or appraiser to value a partner's business interests

☐ How a business is valued as a part of marital property

☐ What to consider when negotiating a buy-out deal

☐ The role that taxes may play

CHAPTER EIGHT

PLANNING YOUR ESTATE

Any woman on her own should have an estate plan pulled together. It doesn't have to be fancy, complicated, or terribly extensive. It all depends on your financial and family situation. But once you've wrangled your way through your partner's estate (either as a result of death or in trying to divide your assets), you can't neglect to address your own.

Being financially independent means that you are solely responsible for making sure your assets are dispersed according to your wishes when you die and that your heirs won't be stuck paying burdensome taxes on what you leave behind. You're also the one who has to decide what will happen to your children should you no longer be able to care for them. For that, you'll want to choose someone to make decisions concerning your estate, your children, and even your own medical care if you are incapacitated.

CHOOSING YOUR ESTATE ATTORNEY

If you are widowed, you may decide to enlist the attorney who settled your partner's estate to help you put your plan together. If you don't already have an estate planning attorney, ask your financial advisor or accountant for recommendations. Ask other attorneys you've worked with on other legal matters such as buying a home for a referral. You can tap into your state or local bar association's website and look for a list of estate specialists in your area. You can also consult the *Martindale-Hubbell Law Directory* (martindale.com). It rates most U.S. attorneys on their ethics. Look for ratings of AV or BV. These are considered to be the top credentials.

Now is the right time to review your property. You probably have turned the corner and are no longer just struggling to get from one day to the next. Knitting together your own long-term financial plan is your next goal, and estate planning is an important part of that strategy. The main question to ask yourself is, "How much do I have at this time and to whom do I want to leave it?" Have this information on hand when you sit down with your estate attorney.

Of course, you probably revised your will immediately after the death of your partner or following your divorce, but you'll want to review it to make certain that what was important to you several months ago still carries the same weight. Your priorities might be somewhat skewed from what they were months ago, and you'll want to make changes in your will to suit those differences.

What does your estate consist of? Simply said, it's the value of assets you leave at the time of your death. This includes insurance policies, investments, retirement funds, your house, and so forth. If you have a beneficiary named already (for example, maybe the assets in your 401(k) plan are assigned to your brother or child), then, of course, those funds will go directly to that individual. Without a will, who gets what and when will be the decision of your state courts. My guess is that how the courts would distribute your assets and how you would do so are not at all the same.

Believe it or not, one of the biggest mistakes people make is in not assigning a beneficiary to their various retirement plans or other investments. When you die, those funds will be taxed and distributed by a court-assigned administrator. In the end, your heirs stand to lose what should rightfully be theirs, and your hard-earned money goes to Uncle Sam.

WRITING A WILL

A will is a legal document stating how you wish your property to be dispersed following your death. It can be pretty simple. Many people even choose to write their own wills. You may find that you can draw up will using a Web-based legal document service such as LegalZoom.com or Nolo.com. But although there is no law requiring you to have a lawyer draw up your will, bypassing professional advice is not always wise. Estate laws can be fairly intricate, and making certain that your will is valid and will hold up in court might require a professional review. Most lawyers will charge you by the hour for their time. In general, a basic will can cost anywhere from $300 to $1,000, and more complicated ones can run to $3,000 or more.

A competent estate attorney can make certain that you don't get anything wrong that can have repercussions for your heirs.

Here are some basic rules for writing a will that will stand up in court.

- First, it must be signed in the presence of at least two and sometimes three witnesses, depending on the laws of the state in which you live.
- Don't ask anyone who is a beneficiary of your property to be a witness. That's a real red flag in terms of validity since it is seen as a conflict of interest.

- If you have been divorced, make sure you remove your ex from any beneficiary clauses. You probably can't do this until your divorce decree is final. You certainly want to strike his or her name from any of your retirement assets or life insurance policies as quickly as you can.
- Your will should clearly state who will inherit what pieces of your property.
- In writing, name the person you have asked to be in charge of making sure your wishes are followed. The person you select to distribute your property is called your **executor**.
- You will have to detail how and when the assets are to be distributed. If you are leaving assets to young children, you might not want them to receive those funds until they reach a certain age; even then, you might want the funds to be paid at intervals instead of all at once. A property guardian is essential, particularly if you have young children, because in most states, children under 18 are not considered legally competent to deal with assets or property worth more than a certain amount—sometimes no more than $5,000. Thus, any inheritance left to your children must be managed by an adult until the children come of age.
- The property guardian can be the same person as your child's guardian. Without a guardian named by you, the court will name one for you and your estate will be divided equally among your children. You should consider naming two separate guardians, one to raise your children and the other to watch over your property. The first person is someone you designate to raise the children in a manner that suits you. The property guardian is someone who is financially savvy and can

take charge of handling the money issues. This should be someone who shares your investment philosophy and can preserve your money for your children and their future educational needs. For example, your sister may have a child-rearing philosophy similar to yours, so you'd feel comfortable having her raise your children. However, she may not be a good money manager or have any interest in investing or managing money, so she might not be the best person to ensure the children's future financial needs by preserving the assets you leave to them.

- Your will should contain your full name, the date, the names of your executor, guardians, and beneficiaries, plus special bequests and trust arrangements.
- Since your estate is likely to grow after you have signed your will, it makes sense to divide the assets in terms of percentages rather than straight dollar amounts. In other words, if you have four children, you might instruct that each will inherit 25 percent of your estate. If you have specific bequests, such as leaving an opal necklace to your niece Caitlin, spell it out clearly in a letter of intent attached to your will to prevent misunderstandings that could cause family discord.

Your next step is to sign the original of the will, and have it witnessed by two adults, and notarized, and store it in a safe place. In this case, a safe-deposit box isn't the ideal place because a state will often seal its contents following a death until the taxes have been figured out. Make sure someone close to you knows where your will is and can find it easily. You may already be aware of the havoc caused by a missing will if your partner died without one or you were unable to locate it quickly. Your lawyer might be willing to keep a signed copy in his or her office.

Your will should be reviewed at regular intervals, maybe every two years, to stay current with your life situation. You should definitely consider making adjustments if there are changes in the tax laws or if you move to another state or remarry.

LIVING WILLS

A living will is a sort of hybrid will that outlines the kind of medical care you want if you are terminally ill. For example, if you don't want to be kept alive on life-support systems, you can make that known. (As morbid as it may seem, this could save your family a substantial sum in medical bills.) In a living will, you can include instructions for organ donation if you wish, and you can designate the person you want to make any medical decisions relating to your care if you are unable to do so.

For a living will to be valid, it must be witnessed by two adults, and they can't be members of your family or medical physicians. You will need to have the document in writing and have it signed and dated and notarized.

DURABLE POWER OF ATTORNEY

A durable power of attorney for finances and for healthcare, or healthcare proxy, are good supplements to a living will. It permits you to name someone to make financial and healthcare decisions for you if you are incapacitated in some way (say, in a coma) but still alive. Your designee can sign checks to pay your bills.

There is no reason you can't have both a living will and a durable power of attorney, and, in fact, you probably should have both. Typically, you would ask a friend or close relative to take on this responsibility. But be sure you have discussed it with them and that they have agreed to do so ahead of time.

Many financial advisors recommend that you have two people designated as powers of attorney, one for medical purposes and one for financial matters. Most states recognize these wills, but the legalities can vary. Make sure the people you pick as your proxies have a copy of the will. As with a living will, the document must be signed, dated, notarized, and witnessed by at least one adult. It should cost you about $100 to have your attorney draw up a power of attorney document for you.

Consider who has your power of attorney to make investment and other financial decisions for you if you're incapacitated. Ask yourself if there is a child who is more financially inclined, or a loved one who can step into that role if necessary, Fidelity's Suzanne Schmitt, vice president for family engagement, advises. "This should be someone you feel comfortable talking about your money with. Somebody who is going to be a health care proxy needs to be a person who is relatively close to you emotionally and physically, she says. "That person is going to have to understand what is important to you."

NAMING AN EXECUTOR

When you write your will, you will name an executor of your estate to make sure disbursement of your assets is carried out according to your wishes. Your executor is responsible for paying debts and distributing what is not already assigned to a beneficiary. Your life insurance policies and retirement plans have probably already been directed to a certain individual.

An executor normally is paid a fee of 3 percent to 5 percent of your total estate. Sometimes, if this person is someone close to you, he or she may opt to pass on the fee. To assign a value to your property, your executor might have to hire an accountant or other professional. Again, make sure the person you name is someone who is willing to take on the task, which can entail a fair amount of time and effort and be emotionally taxing.

TRUSTS TO CONSIDER

A living trust is something you might consider establishing for yourself. You will want to consult an estate planning attorney in order to get the best advice on how to structure a living trust. Basically, you name yourself as the trustee of the trust and designate someone else, maybe your lawyer, as your successor to administer the trust should you become incapacitated because of an illness or accident.

The trust takes effect immediately, and it can be revocable, meaning changes are allowed at any time, or irrevocable, meaning no changes allowed. Basically, with a revocable trust you can retain control. The key advantage is that when you die your heirs receive the assets without having to go through probate, which is the legal process that a court requires to determine if a will is valid and to make sure your property is distributed properly. Probate, believe it or not, can take up to two years for your heirs to battle through and can lop off as much as 10 percent of your estate assets in fees. Unlike probated estates, property that is part of a trust is not a matter of public record when you die; no one can find out what you left to whom, and private matters will stay that way.

To execute a living trust, you will have to rename all your assets in the trust name (for example, the Becky Hackel Trust). The assets that you are renaming will include everything from your savings accounts to any mutual funds you hold.

It's not hard to do this; it just takes a bit of time. You have to write to your bank, mutual fund company, and stockbroker and explain what you are doing. Send the first and last pages of the trust papers and the section that says who has trustee rights. In most cases, you will name yourself, but if you really don't want to worry about financial matters because you are ill or are entangled in some other life crisis, you can name someone else to manage your investments for you.

This doesn't mean you give that person absolute power to invest your money without consulting you. You can outline the exact boundaries of responsibility. The point is that this will be a new account in the trust name, not yours, and you will control it in the same manner you did previously. It's very important to retitle all your assets in the trust name if you want it to hold up in court.

Once you choose to have a living will, you should consider having your attorney attach a **pour-over will**, which allows you to address other matters, such as naming a guardian for your children and designating who should get what in terms of physical possessions.

NAMING A TRUSTEE

You need to name someone to be the trustee of your trust when you die. Since this is a job that may take more than a year or two and is all about money, you should pick someone with expertise in the field of finance and money management. Because this can be a complicated and long-term project, you might want to hammer out a deal with a bank's trust department or an investment firm to manage this service. Typically, they will charge an annual fee of up to 1.5 percent of the value of the assets under their management.

It's important to divulge your estate plan to a friend or close relative. Your attorney may be tops, but someone closer to you needs to understand what you have in mind. That way, if someone contests the will, there will be an advocate to fight for your wishes. Make sure this individual knows where you have filed your will and whom to call (your lawyer, perhaps) if there is a crisis.

In Chapter Nine, we'll learn about what to do when you're ready to move on to another relationship.

CHAPTER RECAP

In this chapter, we have learned:

☐ Why you should have a will that you regularly review
☐ What is the purpose of a power of attorney
☐ What is the role of a guardian
☐ When and how to set up a trust

CHAPTER NINE

MOVING ON

Even if you are a single woman today, chances are good that you will find another partner. Certainly, there is nothing wrong with moving on with your life. Wanting to have someone to share with is natural. For many women, that new partner may have also been divorced or widowed. Many widows find new mates through a surviving partner's support group—the companionship and shared experience of grief forms a strong bond.

When you are emotionally ready to consider remarriage, however, there are important money issues to consider. You have worked so hard to establish your own financial identity and to learn to manage your money solo that it's critical to look out for your own financial independence. As unromantic as it may seem, even the most loving marriages include a lot more than hearts and roses.

Marriage is at its very roots a financial partnership. The best marriages are about sharing and love, but they are also a money partnership. If you want to save yourself heartbreak and financial loss should your next marriage end in divorce or widowhood, it should be treated as an equal financial partnership from the start.

You can't risk losing the money left to you by your late partner or from your divorce settlement by plunging carelessly

into a starry-eyed relationship. You don't have to have a trea-
sure chest or vast fortune to opt for a prenuptial agreement.
Separating your emotions from your money is a key factor in
protecting yourself against disaster.

Years ago, it was unheard of to discuss the indelicate
topic of money before that stroll down the aisle. Signing a
prenuptial agreement seemed to say that you didn't trust your
future partner or that you weren't really in it for the long haul.
But those days are over. It's no longer insulting to talk about
money before you say "I do." It's just plain smart.

WHAT IS A PRENUP?

Simply put, a prenup is a document or pact signed before your
marriage that spells out how your assets will be divided in the
event of death or divorce. Some people even use it as a plan for
how all finances will be managed during their marriage. Some
agreements go as far as to require that the partner maintain a
regular sexual relationship with the other partner in order to
be eligible for any portion of assets. Anything goes. But the
important thing is that you discuss your financial lives openly
before you remarry. If the partner you are planning to marry
has been married before or widowed, he or she may have
children to rear. They may also have debts you know nothing
about. You need to decide how you want to share your two sets
of assets.

There is no need to feel obligated to join your financial
lives together in a formal manner. Most financial advisors
argue that mingling assets by including your new partner on
the title of your house or by adding his or her name to your
investments can lead to nothing but trouble, particularly if the
new partner has fewer assets than you do. To ensure that your

hard-earned financial stability holds firm, it's advisable to sign a prenup.

The idea of signing a marriage agreement that concerns financial matters isn't really new at all. Jewish marriage ceremonies have included the act of signing the *ketubah* for centuries. The *ketubah* is a Hebrew pact that defines a husband's obligations to his bride. It covers everything from providing clothes and food to sexual relations. It also states that the husband is responsible for providing a set amount of money for his wife should he leave her through divorce or death.

Writing a prenuptial agreement might cost you a few thousand dollars depending on how complicated it is, but it is a step worth taking for most women marrying for the second time.

WHY YOU NEED A MIDLIFE PRENUP IF YOU'RE PLANNING A NEW MARRIAGE

Popping the P-word. If you're planning to get married again, whether it'll be your first marriage or your fourth, there's a good chance you'll want to have a prenuptial agreement. You've likely accumulated some wealth in a 401(k) retirement plan and IRAs, probably own a home, and might even run a business. And you may have children from a previous marriage. All these factors make a prenup extremely helpful.

Simply put, a prenup spells out how your financial assets—including real estate, cars, savings, and investments—will be doled out when the marriage ends, either in divorce or with the death of a partner. A prenup can indicate who'll be responsible for outstanding debts. It can even determine who'll get custody of your Labrador retriever.

WHAT CAN HAPPEN WITHOUT A PRENUP

Without a prenup, if you divorce, you can be legally required to divide the property you brought into the marriage in a manner that doesn't suit you. You might have to pay alimony—more and more women do these days. And your new life partner may have debts that you could be responsible for paying. If you die without a prenup, your partner might be able to legally claim up to half of your assets.

If you don't have a prenup and can't come to an agreement during divorce proceedings, your state laws will dictate division of the assets. That means that in community-property states (currently Arizona, California, Idaho, Louisiana, Nevada, New Mexico, Texas, Washington, and Wisconsin), you'll probably get half of everything. But in other states, assets will be split by the court depending on factors such as how long you were married and what you accumulated together.

Drawing up a prenuptial agreement isn't just for the rich and famous anymore. More and more boomers preparing to tie the knot are heading to lawyers, who often charge a few thousand dollars to draw up a prenup.

Over the years, though, the knee-jerk negative reaction to asking for a prenup has dissipated. Prenups are now part of our culture. If you're contemplating marriage, I strongly recommend you consider a prenup if you fall into one or more of these categories:

- You're bringing $100,000 or more in assets to the partnership.
- You have children from a prior relationship.
- You own or co-own a business.
- You earn a hefty salary (or are likely to do so in the future).

PRENUPS ARE NOT ROMANTIC

Although more common than ever, asking a potential partner to sign a prenup can still be dicey.

"Whoever brings it up is considered to be extremely unromantic," says Olivia Mellan, a psychotherapist and money coach based in Washington, D.C. The whole prenup process can be polluted by resentments, anger, and the fallout of painful former relationships.

But marriage is in many respects a business deal. And a prenup is just one of the legal documents that seal the deal.

CREATING AN IRON-CLAD AGREEMENT

- You and your partner should each hire a lawyer. This will ensure that you each have an advocate in your corner. Thousands of attorneys who specialize in matrimonial law handle prenups. If you don't know one, ask for recommendations from friends, family members, or the attorney who drew up your will.
- Full disclosure is vital. Both you and your future partner must come clean about all your finances, including assets, income, and debts.
- Be sure you're both willing to sign the document. You usually need two witnesses and must sign the prenup well in advance of the marriage so neither partner can say it was done under duress. Two or three months before the wedding date is ideal.
- Agree on any waivers in advance. If you want your kids to receive your 401(k) or pension when you die, your partner will need to turn over his or her rights to the money by filing a waiver

with the plan trustee after your wedding. Be sure
your prenup includes an agreement to file the
waiver. (IRA proceeds always go to your named
beneficiary, regardless of what's in a prenup or
will.)

- If you have adult children, talk with them about
the prenup before you sign it. Your children
may believe that any money you have left when
you die belongs rightfully to them and not a
new partner. They may also have other financial
concerns about your re-marriage, so it's wise to
give them a chance to weigh-in.

HOW TO MAKE A PRENUP HOLD UP IN COURT

The key to making these agreements successful is to begin
by each of you hiring your own lawyer. There are thousands
of attorneys who specialize in matrimonial law and handle
prenups frequently. You don't want your new partner to be
able to argue that there was any type of conflict of interest.

Both you and your future partner must divulge detailed
financial information, including all assets, income, and debts.
Full disclosure is paramount. Then the pact must be signed
voluntarily by both of you and far enough in advance of your
wedding day so neither partner can claim it was signed under
duress. Two or three months ahead of your wedding date is
advisable, as I mentioned above. And it's probably a good idea
to film/record the signing so you have a record. If there are bad
feelings about signing a prenup, you might consider setting a
future date on which the contract will expire.

POSTNUPTIAL AGREEMENTS

If you don't have a prenup and can't come to an agreement with your ex-partner during the divorce proceedings, your state laws will dictate division of the assets. That means that in the community-property states of Arizona, California, Idaho, Louisiana, Nevada, New Mexico, Texas, Washington, and Wisconsin, you will probably get half of everything. In other states, assets will be split by the court depending on factors such as how long you were married and what you actually accumulated together.

It's never too late to draw up an agreement, even after you have been married for a while. A postnuptial agreement is just as valid as a prenup and is set up the same way. You should seriously consider this option if you inherit a lump sum of money or have a large cash infusion from selling a business.

These agreements will hold up in court if they are written properly. Never lose sight of your goal: keeping your financial independence. If the man or woman you want to marry is unwilling to sign an agreement, you should probably take some time to think things through.

Be pragmatic when it comes to linking your life to a new person. Living happily ever after doesn't always happen for most of us. You've learned that the hard way. It takes time to recover from the loss of a partner, so take it slowly and be honest with yourself. But never forget that being responsible for your own finances and striving to constantly educate yourself about money issues will give you the confidence and freedom to survive these life-shattering blows. Taking control of your financial life is a necessity.

With your financial plan firmly in place, handling money will become a routine part of your daily life. The most difficult work is behind you.

CHAPTER RECAP

In this chapter, we have learned:

☐ What a prenuptial agreement entails
☐ How to ensure the prenup will hold up in court
☐ When the prenup should be written

KERRY'S MONEY-SAVVY CHECKLIST

Here's how to stay on-board for a financially secure future by the decades.

TWENTIES TO THIRTIES

- ☐ **Learn the money basics.** Two books to consider: *How to Think About Money* by Jonathan Clements and *Get A Financial Life: Personal Finance in Your Twenties and Thirties* by Beth Kobliner. The Investor Protection Institute's site, iInvest.org, offers free guides that explain stocks, bonds, and mutual funds. You might also opt to take a personal finance course at a community college or check for online offerings on sites such as Coursera.org.

- ☐ **Sketch out your monthly budget.** Add up the fundamentals—your rent or mortgage, utilities, groceries, transportation, student loans, and car loans—and subtract from your monthly after-tax pay. Websites such as Mint.com and YouNeedABudget.com offer free software to track spending, set up a budget, and more.

- ☐ **Avoid credit card debt.** Debt can haunt you for years to come, from securing a mortgage down the road to even getting hired, because employers are known to check potential employees' credit reports as part of their due diligence.

□ **Start saving and investing.** Take advantage of your employer's 401(k) or similar retirement plan. Contributions are tax-deductible, and investments grow tax-deferred until withdrawals in retirement. Invest enough in your 401(k) to qualify for the full match (the amount your employer puts in as a result of how much you contribute). Most employers require workers to save between 4 percent to 6 percent of pay to get the maximum match. Begin by saving at least 5 percent of your salary and increase the amount by 1 percent every year until you reach 20 percent. Some plans allow participants to schedule automatic increases each year.

□ **Diversify investments.** Aim for a portfolio of stocks or stock mutual funds. Over time, equities outperform returns on fixed income investments. Investors more than fifteen years from retirement should consider an aggressive portfolio with more than 80 percent allocated to stocks, since they provide the long-term growth potential you will need.

□ **Invest in a diverse mix of low-cost index funds.** You might select a trio of funds: a broad U.S. stock market index fund; an international stock market index with exposure to both developed and emerging markets; and an index fund that owns the overall U.S. bond market.

□ **Target-date funds (TDFs) or balanced mutual funds that invest in stocks and bonds.** This fund type automatically adjusts the balance of fixed income investments and stocks based on your age.

☐ **Contribute to a Roth IRA.** If you earn enough and have money to save outside of that plan and don't earn so much that you are capped out by the IRS income limitations, contribute to a Roth IRA.

☐ **Review your credit report.** The three credit bureaus—Experian, TransUnion, and Equifax—provide one free report annually. To request one, go to AnnualCreditReport.com. Build this yearly checkup into your routine for the rest of your life to keep an eye on any mistakes that can trip you up down the road when you need access to credit.

☐ **Don't skip health insurance.** Currently, you can be insured as a dependent on your parent's health insurance plan if you're under twenty-six. The exception: If you can get health insurance through your own job. If you can't piggyback onto your parent's plan and you don't have a job with health insurance, you might need to buy a short-term policy through a health insurance marketplace.

☐ **Start an emergency fund.** This is cash that is available to cover unreimbursed medical bills or auto or home repairs. A year's worth of expenses is your ultimate goal.

☐ **Start a money book club or a money-circle discussion group.** A club can force you to read useful books you might never have picked up on your own. A money-circle group lets you and your friends hold regular conversations about finances and help each other.

FORTIES

☐ **Build a relationship with a financial advisor.**
You should seek a fee-only financial planner who
has the Certified Financial Planner designation,
awarded by the nonprofit Certified Financial
Planner Board of Standards. Three national groups
of financial planners offer searchable databases
with contact information: The National Association
of Personal Financial Advisors, The Financial
Planning Association, and the Certified Financial
Planner Board of Standards.

☐ **Rebalance your retirement account regularly.**
Financial advisors normally suggest rebalancing
whenever your portfolio gets more than 7 percent
to 10 percent from your original asset allocation
between equities and fixed income—both
international and domestic.

☐ **Make a personal retirement plan projection.** A
good place to start is the online calculator called
the Ballpark E$timate, from the Employee Benefit
Research Institute's site, www.choosetosave.org.
Many major mutual fund companies also have
good retirement calculators on their sites.

☐ **Insure yourself.** If you have children or other
dependents, most financial professionals
recommend a term life insurance policy that
provides hundreds of thousands of dollars of
coverage for minimum premiums over terms of
twenty or thirty years, but has no cash value.

☐ **Set up a self-employed retirement plan.** If you're
starting a business, or moving to a nonprofit or a

small firm without an employee retirement plan, you should keep setting aside money as long as possible in tax-friendly accounts. Your three main options: a SEP-IRA, Solo 401(k), and a SIMPLE IRA. One of the biggest mistakes entrepreneurs make is not planning adequately—or at all—for their retirement.

FIFTIES

☐ **Pay down debt.** If possible, pay off outstanding high-interest credit card debts, college loans, and auto loans. Debt can be a real dream killer. So the earlier you can start to get a grip on this, the better off you'll be when your prime earning years fade.

☐ **Make your catch-up contributions.** If you've fallen behind, now's the time to play catch-up. Workers fifty and older currently can contribute around $6,000 in "catch-up" contributions to their 401(k) or other employer-provided retirement plans.

☐ **Review your Social Security and pension benefit options.** You can get an estimate of your future Social Security benefits and a record of your lifetime earnings history at ssa.gov. The AARP website, aarp.org, also has a retirement and a Social Security Benefits calculator. These days, many people elect to begin claiming Social Security as soon as they turn sixty-two, the earliest age they can. If you delay claiming Social Security from age

sixty-two to seventy, you will increase benefits by
about 8 percent a year.

☐ **Start planning your next act.** If you want to start
an encore career in your next chapter, keep in mind
that money is the biggest stumbling block when
it comes to changing careers later in life. That's
because starting over in a new field, particularly
a philanthropic one, or going the self-employment
route usually comes with a price tag, at least
initially. Start planning a few years ahead of time
by saving, adding new skills, and downsizing.

☐ **Make a move.** Investigate the upside of moving to
a smaller home, townhouse, or condo. Depending
on your real estate market, refinancing your
mortgage can also lighten your debt load. Figure
out how much you can save over time with an
online refinancing calculator. Check HSH.com or
Bankrate.com for the latest rates and then shop
around.

☐ **Protect the wealth you've created.** Review
disability, life, personal liability, and umbrella
insurance. Evaluate long-term care insurance
coverage (generally not appropriate before or
after mid-fifties). Premiums get much larger as
you age, and if you have any health issues it
might disqualify you. Update your will and estate
planning documents. Watch out for high mutual
fund and management fees. These can whittle away
your savings dramatically over time.

SIXTIES AND BEYOND

☐ **Get a grip on your retirement income sources.** Sit down at least a year before you stop working and look carefully at anticipated income (Social Security benefits, any pensions, distributions from personal investments, and savings) and expenses (weekly, monthly, and yearly budgets).

☐ **Take control of fixed monthly costs**. Downsize. Consider selling your home, if you own one, or moving to an area with a lower cost of living, and moving to a rental property. This will allow you to save a bundle in property taxes, maintenance, and insurance costs. Some people who live in high cost-of-living areas might look at relocating to an area with lower taxes and cheaper real estate costs.

☐ **Consider working beyond your official retirement age.** The more earning years you can build savings in a defined contribution plan like a 401(k), the better. It can also provide income to pay for health insurance until you're eligible for Medicare at sixty-five. If you're lucky, your job offers you access to a health plan.

☐ **Shift your investments to a more conservative asset mix**. You may, however, still want to hang on to, say, 40 percent stock holdings well into retirement.

☐ **Plan your withdrawal rates.** A conservative annual drawdown of your savings is, say, 3 percent in the first year, plus an annual adjustment for inflation.

148

For example, if you have saved $1 million when you retire, you can withdraw $30,000 in the first year from your portfolio and increase that amount by 3 percent in the second year, and so on.

MOVING ON: A MONEY CHECKLIST

☐ **Find a trustworthy financial advisor.** He or she can help answer your questions and lend a sharp eye to your total financial picture. For unbiased guidance, look for a fee-only planner with the Certified Financial Planner designation or an Accredited Financial Counselor (AFC.) You can find one by visiting sites of the National Association of Personal Financial Advisors, the Financial Planning Association and the Certified Financial Planner Board of Standards. Another excellent source of financial advice is the Association for Financial Counseling and Education (AFCPE. org) website. An Accredited Financial Counselor can address your immediate money challenge and help you create a plan to achieve your goals. You can search by location and area of expertise. Fees typically start around $200 an hour, but vary. Virtual sessions are possible.

☐ **Make a personal retirement plan projection.** Start with the Ballpark E$timate online calculator from the Employee Benefit Research Institute's site, choosetosave.org. Many major mutual fund companies also have good retirement calculators on their sites.

☐ **Get estimates of your future Social Security and pension benefits.** If you haven't already, set up your "my Social Security account" at SocialSecurity.gov for an estimate of your future

Social Security benefits and a record of your lifetime earnings history. There are several online services to help you decide when to claim Social Security, including Social Security's retirement estimator (ssa.gov/retire/estimator.html), T. Rowe Price's Social Security Benefits Evaluator (http://individual.troweprice.com/public/Retail/ Retirement/Social-Security-Tool), and AARP's Social Security calculator (aarp.org/work/social-security/social-security-benefits-calculator). The Pension Rights Center (PensionRights.org) can answer pension questions free of charge.

☐ **Read your Social Security benefit statements**. Paper mailings go out every five years to American workers aged twenty-five and older who haven't registered for "My Social Security." After you turn sixty, printed statements are sent annually. Reading your Social Security statement can remind you how much you need to save for retirement and propel you to begin figuring out when to start claiming Social Security benefits.

☐ **Pencil out retirement living costs**. The Bestplaces. net site has a handy calculator to compare locations around the U.S. Think about moving to a smaller home, townhouse, or condo. Refinancing your mortgage might also lighten your debt load; use an online refinancing calculator at HSH.com or Bankrate.com and shop for the best rates.

☐ **Rebalance your retirement account regularly**. Rebalancing is a strategy for returning your investment portfolio to the mix of stocks and bonds matching your risk tolerance and goals. Your

401(k) plan may offer an auto-rebalancing option. Otherwise, consider using a robo-advisor—an online money manager, such as wealthfront.com and Betterment.com or Ellevest (ellevest.com).

☐ **Plan your retirement plan withdrawal rate.** A conservative annual drawdown of your savings is 3 percent in the first year of retirement, plus an annual adjustment for inflation.

☐ **Prepare for an encore career.** For advice on a second act that'll provide purpose and a paycheck, go to Encore.org. Four excellent books that can also help you get started: *The Encore Career Handbook: How to Make a Living and a Difference in the Second Half of Life*, *Great Jobs for Everyone 50+: Finding Work That Keeps You Happy and Healthy ... And Pays the Bills*, *Second-Act Careers: 50+ Ways to Profit from Your Passions During Semi-Retirement*, and *Unretirement: How Baby Boomers Are Changing the Way We Think About Work, Community, and the Good Life*.

☐ **Write or update your will.** If you die without a will, there's no guarantee who will inherit your assets. What's more, your estate will go into probate, a costly, slow-moving legal process. Hire an estate lawyer to draft your will; if your assets are in the six figures or higher, you probably ought to have a trust as well, to help minimize estate taxes and avoid probate. A trust also offers you greater control over when and how your assets will be distributed.

☐ **Update your beneficiaries.** If your beneficiaries are out-of-date, when you die, your assets could go to the wrong person—your ex-partner, for example. To make sure the money in your 401(k) and other retirement accounts will wind up in the right hands after you die, check to be sure your beneficiary designations are current. Go to the site of the financial services firm where you hold your accounts and update the information online.

☐ **Get your financial and estate planning documents together.** Create a file for them: your will (and trusts if you have them); a durable power of attorney form that gives someone the ability to make financial decisions for you if you can't; and your end-of life instructions, such as a living will and health-care power of attorney. Also, include all your credit card and other financial accounts with their numbers and passwords. Store this all in a safe place, but be sure a loved one knows where, for when the time comes.

PARTING WORDS

You've got this. Breathe and believe. I wrote this book specifically as a plain, by-the-bootstraps guide to getting your money feet back on the ground, because I know the heart part is something a book simply can't heal.

As you've read from the women who've shared their personal lives with you in these pages, being on your own is a unique journey for everyone. At the root of a money-confident woman is your attitude, outlook, and willingness to learn, ask questions, and be patient with yourself.

You will absorb knowledge and adapt to your new circumstances and, in time, thrive. Life continues, and you will be an active participant in all aspects of it—mind, body, and soul.

If you have followed some of the lessons I've shared in these pages, you've already pushed outside your comfort zone. It's a process. It takes some gumshoe work.

Opportunities are rarely handed to you. You have to go out and get your hands in the dirt to achieve it.

Like most challenges in life that we face, there's no ideal starting point. You need to just make that phone call to ask for help, enroll in a class to learn about personal finance. When we shift to learning mode, we begin to reengage in the world again.

Living in the past and mourning your old life as a couple will make you feel stuck. Focus on the actions you can take today. How you deal with setbacks echoes throughout your life.

Set tiny, precise goals for yourself. Consider creating a vision board for motivation. Cut up photos from publications and glue them to a poster board of things that you want to achieve, or places you want to go, or what makes you happy. You can also download them from Pinterest and Google Images and make a computer document or create a screensaver from the images for your computer.

Design one and put it somewhere you can see it on a regular basis, and let your mind go there for a few minutes each day to reflect and dream.

Reframe negative self-talk by shifting your thinking, for example, from, "I'm not good with money" to, "I love to learn about investing and saving." Negativity eats away at your confidence. Be mindful of the language that runs through your mind, or words you say out loud, that degrades your ability to manage your money with self-assurance and poise. Replace it with positive words of action verbs.

Be kind to yourself. This is time to energize and rebuild. It's not a time for blaming others for your circumstances or self-pity. You can't get stuck in a moment.

Follow my HOVER Approach. HOVER stands for the five core ingredients you must have, or will need to develop, to create change in your life.

Hope is essential. When you have confidence that you can reach your goals, you will find a way to do so.

Optimism allows you to have a positive approach, which helps you keep pushing ahead even when there are roadblocks.

Value means knowing that you have the skills and intelligence to get results and make progress, if you put out the effort.

Enthusiasm is the intangible "oomph" factor that provides the energy needed to make those necessary changes, both internally and externally.

Resilience, the knack for springing back in the face of adversity or failure, is indispensable to achieve happiness. Mental resilience allows you to show mettle in the face of adversity.

One of my favorite sayings is, "Focus on what you can do, not what you can't." I have found that these are the reasons why women are great investors and money managers:

- Women are apt to take their time and do a lot of research before making an investment decision. No rash moves.
- As Diane Harris, former editor-in-chief of MONEY and co-author of *It Takes Money, Honey*, a personal finance book for women, told me that women really like to feel that we understand what we're doing. I'm going to make a gross generalization here, but unlike men—who might occasionally take a stock tip on the golf course—women are not going to pick up a stock tip from somebody who's, say, coloring our roots.
- We're more patient in waiting for returns.
- We ask advice from others in hopes of finding a consensus.
- We're more likely to see investing as part of a long-term planning process to achieve a goal rather than

as a contest or competition. Men's investments can actually suffer from overconfidence. Male investors tend to swing for the fences; they think they can beat the market. That bravado, which tends to result in more trading in and out of the market, doesn't really serve them well. Women are less likely to jump out of stocks in times of stress.

Women are tough and resilient far beyond what we imagine. So many times, we get caught up in what we think we can or cannot do. Stop the mental chatter.

Do something every day to work toward your goal. Keep in mind, though, that while setting goals is inspiring, exhilarating, and challenging, the devil is in the details. If you focus on the small moves while in pursuit of that goal, studies show you'll be more successful.

Along the way, it's important to recognize and celebrate your hard work and dedication to stay on track. You might want to keep a journal to track your progress on a regular basis and ways to keep yourself accountable to laying the groundwork to a rich life. List daily things that you're grateful for that day, things that went right, what you learned.

Set goals, short- and long-term, to design your rich financial future. Write down what it would look like to be financially confident in ideal scenarios. What money-smart women do you admire, for example? Why? Who do you not want to be like?

Jot down what kinds of jobs do these women hold or held, what sorts of investments they hold, how do they dress, where do they live, what causes do they support?

This is your playbook journal for financial and life success. It can be cathartic and self-affirming. "You've got to dream to get there," was a refrain my father always said to me.

Once you have your vision of the end result through your vision board and this journal, you can start your journey. It becomes a magnet. This process works whether it's achieving a professional goal, or overcoming a more personal obstacle, such as a health crisis or personal trauma such as a divorce or the death of a partner.

Shift your mind-set from failure and inadequacy to accomplishment and possibility. The key is to not let any doubt trash those goals you're planting today. It's your long-term point of view to remember.

If you want to become a money-confident woman badly enough, you will find a way to make it happen. The only way to get stronger—physically, financially, and mentally—is realizing that the core strength is already inside of you.

Being responsible for your financial well-being is up to you, but as I said repeatedly in this book, you don't have to fly solo.

Build your expert team who have your best interests at heart and will motivate you. Many women feel financial advisors don't "get" them. Some women don't work with money pros, however, because they feel they don't have sufficient assets or the advisors' fees are too high. There's a big misconception that you have to have a certain amount of assets or income, or I'll have to pay a huge price to hire a financial advisor.

My advice: Stop making excuses. Some do take middle-income clients and have reasonable fees for a session or two to get you started. Interview a few. Find one you like and then don't be shy about asking the questions you need to make sense of it all.

Use online money-management tools and calculators. Dive into the electronic arena to ramp up your investing savvy. Online tools are a great way to learn and to save time dealing with your financial life.

Your employer's resources are another good place to start. The Employer-Sponsored Health and Well-Being Survey from the National Business Group on Health and Fidelity Investments found that 84 percent of 141 large- and mid-sized companies surveyed now have financial wellness programs. They offer seminars and "lunch-n-learn" programs and resources to support emergency savings, debt management and budgeting, student loan counseling or repayment assistance. Personalized financial counseling is also growing fast, according to the latest study from Financial Finesse, a provider of employer financial-wellness programs.

Taking a Scarlett O'Hara ("Tomorrow is another day") approach toward your financial future is unwise. A Fidelity survey found that eight in ten women said they avoid financial conversations because they are "too personal" or "uncomfortable." The report also found that women are more likely to talk with significant others in their lives about health issues and sex than wealth, salary or investment ideas.

There is no one right way to do this. Becoming a money-confident woman is about transformation and investing in our future and ourselves and enjoying the life we have right now (within reason) while setting our course for a prosperous endgame.

Stick with your plain-vanilla strategy. That's what millionaires do, and don't let market swings or hot performance sway you. Pay greater attention to the small stuff that can nick returns over time.

Remember that passively managed index funds and ETFs outpace actively managed funds over the long term, thanks to their lower costs. To improve your self-control, automate your investing as much as possible.

Complacency is your enemy. Dig down into the money trenches. It's honestly what helped me pay attention to my finances and take charge. Daily habits can separate well-off people from the not-so-well-off. Have a to-do list and stick to it. Even if there are only a few items on that list, complete each task before the end of the day.

Leave doubt at the door. *Nothing* can stop you. You must push further to progress to the next level. It probably means making tough choices about where and how to spend your money.

Don't set limits! Don't let anyone tell you what you can and cannot accomplish. You are only limited by your own imagination, my father always told me.

Think of your life as Me Inc. *You* are the boss. You make the rules, set the pace, and make the decisions.

So dream b*ig*! Always seek to raise the bar, and then go after it with every ounce of your being.

Finally, I would be remiss if I did not mention my signature Kerry's Fitness Plan. To become a money-confident woman:

- **Get financially fit:** Find ways to get lean and mean. When you're financially fit, possibilities open for you to try new things, to shift into new areas of work, perhaps, to have the time to volunteer for causes you care about, to follow your passions. You're nimble. Debt is a dream killer.
- **Get physically fit.** You don't have to run fast miles or bench press, but walk a mile or two regularly. I walk my dog, Zena, a few miles a day. You might swim. Your choice. But get moving. Eat nutritiously. When you're fit, you are more positive, optimistic. You have a can-do spirit.
- **Get spiritually fit.** I'm not talking whoo whoo religion, but rather find a place to center yourself. This is a stressful time in your life. You might consider a yoga practice, mediation, tai chi. Whatever, it is, find something to do that can help you de-stress, and focus, and find balance, so you can prepare to move down this path with grace.

It's time to make really smart financial moves, let's go!

TEST YOUR INVESTING MOJO

Think you have a good handle on saving, investing, debt, and Social Security? Here's a quick and easy way to gauge your money-management acumen. Take this 10-question, multiple-choice quiz that I created for NextAvenue.org to find out. The scoring is at the end.

1. **You should save regularly for retirement and other long-term financial goals with an amount that matches at least ...**
   a) 3 percent of your net income
   b) 5 percent of your net income
   c) 10 percent of your net income

2. **Generally speaking, you should have enough money set aside to pay living expenses for a minimum of ...**
   a) one month
   b) three months
   c) one year

3. **Your total debt (not including your mortgage) should be no more than ...**
   a) 10 percent of your net income
   b) 35 percent of your net income
   c) 45 percent of your net income

4. **The best way to raise your credit score is to ...**
   a) pay your bills on time
   b) cancel your credit cards
   c) apply for credit on a regular basis

5. **You should update your will ...**
    a) when you have a major life change, such as
    marriage, divorce, death of a partner or spouse, or
    birth of a child
    b) when your child graduates from college
    c) when you get a financial windfall

6. **If you are divorced, you are typically eligible
    for your ex's Social Security benefit if ...**
    a) you were married for at least five years
    b) you're sixty-two or older, were married for at
    least ten years, and are not currently married
    c) your ex-partner lets you have it

7. **If you leave a company before you have
    "vested" in your employer-sponsored 401(k)
    plan, you ...**
    a) always lose any amount your employer contributed
    b) receive the full amount of your contributions
    and your employer's
    c) might receive a percentage of your employer's
    contributions in addition to your own

8. **The best way to determine how much you'll
    need to have saved to cover retirement living
    expenses is to ...**
    a) calculate how much you spend annually now
    and multiply that by the number of years you
    think you will live after you retire
    b) plan on about 70 percent of your current costs
    multiplied out for your retirement years
    c) make a personal retirement plan projection

9. **Every woman needs ...**
   a) a living will
   b) a healthcare power of attorney and a financial
   power of attorney
   c) both a and b

10. **The biggest hurdle to realizing financial well-
    being in retirement is ...**
    a) you haven't penciled out a budget
    b) the unpredictable stock market
    c) you haven't started a regular savings strategy
    that includes investing in stocks and bonds

ANSWER KEY

Give yourself 10 points for each correct answer.

1. Answer: C, 10 percent of your net income.

The least painful way is to contribute automatically to an employer's retirement plan or saving
through payroll deductions. It's the out-of-sight,
out-of-mind method of saving. If you have put
off saving until age fifty, you'll probably need to
save closer to 20 percent to retire well.

2. Answer: B, three months.

It's vital to have an emergency savings cushion in
case you, or someone in your family, encounters
unexpected, uninsured medical costs, or you lose

your job. Target three times your basic monthly expenses to get started, but if you can ramp it up to a year's worth of savings over time, do so. A money market mutual fund and a bank savings account are smart, safe places to safeguard this money.

3. Answer: B, no more than 35 percent of your net income.

Lenders look at your debt-to-income ratio—the amount of debt you have versus your overall income—when they are deciding whether to extend credit, say, to approve you for a mortgage or a credit card. Generally, the lower it is, the greater the chance you will be approved. Check out a debt-to-income ratio calculator. BankRate.com has one.

4. Answer: A, pay your bills on time.

Approximately 35 percent of your credit score is based on your payment history, according to Fair Isaac Corporation, whose FICO score is the most widely used. Around 30 percent is based on how much credit you have access to and how much you're using; about 15 percent is based on how long you've had your credit cards; and roughly 10 percent is determined by the number of times credit card companies request your credit report. (Lots of requests suggest you may be desperate for credit and headed for trouble.)

5. Answer: A, when you have a major life change, such as marriage, divorce, death of a partner or spouse, or birth of a child.

The point of a will is to ensure that the right people will inherit your assets. So, getting married or divorced or having a baby are all good reasons to get your will updated. Without a will, there's no telling who'll get what you leave. Plus, your estate will go into probate—a costly, slow-moving legal process. If your assets are in the six figures or higher, you probably ought to have a trust as well, to help minimize estate taxes and avoid probate.

6. Answer: B, you're sixty-two or older, were married for at least ten years, and are not currently married.

Don't pass up your ex's Social Security benefit if you're entitled. You may be eligible to collect as much as half of your partner's Social Security retirement or disability benefits, even if he has remarried. (If you remarry, though, you generally cannot collect Social Security benefits on your former partner's record unless your later marriage ends by death, divorce or annulment.) You may also be able to receive only your ex's Social Security benefits now and delay receiving your own until a later date, which is a great idea. Social Security benefits are increased by a certain percentage—8 percent annually for those born after 1943—if you delay your retirement beyond Full Retirement Age, now sixty-six to sixty-seven.

7. Answer: C, might receive a percentage of your employer's contributions in addition to your own. In a plan like a 401(k), your contributions and any subsequent earnings are always 100 percent vested. However, you may have to work a set number of years before you are vested in the employer's matching contributions. For example, with graduated vesting, an employee must be at least 20 percent vested after two years, 40 percent after three years, 60 percent after four years, 80 percent after five years, and 100 percent after six years.

8. Answer: C, make a personal retirement plan projection.

Knowledge is power. Once you have your plan in place, you begin to take action and can see your stockpile accumulating year after year. Workers who have done a retirement savings needs calculation tend to report higher savings goals and are more likely to feel very confident about affording a comfortable retirement. Start with the Ballpark E$timate calculator from the Employee Benefit Research Institute's site, Choose to Save (choosetosave.org/ballpark). Many mutual fund companies also have useful retirement calculators on their sites.

9. Answer: C, both a living will and a healthcare power of attorney and a financial power of attorney.

A living will stipulates your end-of-life wishes. A healthcare power of attorney names the person who will make healthcare decisions for you if you can't. A financial power of attorney names the person who will make money decisions for you if you can't. One of the major benefits of having these papers in place is that you save your family the angst of trying to guess what you'd want. It can also avoid family conflicts and a significant financial burden on your heirs.

10. Answer: C, you haven't started a regular savings strategy that includes investing in stocks and bonds.

One key to a comfortable retirement is putting a disciplined, diversified investing plan in place in advance. Bonds generally are less volatile than stocks, but over the long haul, stocks have outperformed bonds, bank savings accounts, and CDs. A general guideline for a safe, diversified retirement savings portfolio: take one hundred and subtract your age for the percentage of your portfolio to hold in stocks. If you're fifty-five, you'd want 45 percent in stocks. As you get older, gradually shift toward a higher concentration in safer bonds.

100 points: Congratulations! You have your financial wits about you. But never stop learning about ways to manage your money. Continue to make your finances a priority, and you should be well-prepared for a secure future.

70 to 90 points: This is pretty darn good. You have the basics under your belt and are on your way. Keep at it, though. Push yourself to focus with a vengeance and stay on top of your money game by regularly monitoring your situation.

40 to 60 points: You've learned a few important things about taking control of your finances, but you need to ramp it up. A good way to get started is to scan the list of stories in Next Avenue's special section and see where you can learn more. Also, do the intermediate checklist.

0 to 30 points: Yikes! It's time for you to start learning about investing and putting money aside for your retirement.

GLOSSARY

ADJUSTED GROSS INCOME This is your bottom-line income on which your federal income tax is computed. It's computed by subtracting certain expenses and other allowable adjustments (e.g., contributions to IRAs) from your gross income.

ALIMONY Funds paid to an ex-partner as required by a legally binding separation agreement or divorce decree. Alimony is taxable income to the partner who receives it.

AMERICAN DEPOSITORY RECEIPTS (ADRS) Receipts for shares of foreign-based companies traded on U.S. stock exchanges. ADRs, or dollar-dominated securities, are the equivalent of a certain number of company shares.

ANNUITY This is a type of investment in which you or your partner, as policyholders, make payments to an insurance company. The money grows tax-free until you withdraw it at retirement. It earns interest and pays a death benefit.

ASSET What you actually own, such as your home, a car, jewelry, and anything else that has monetary value.

ASSET ALLOCATION This is how you apportion your investments in your portfolio. You might own a mix of international mutual funds, large-company stock funds, bonds, and money market funds.

BALANCED MUTUAL FUNDS These are mutual funds invested in a mix of stocks and bonds, usually 60 percent in stocks and the remainder in bonds.

BALANCE SHEET This is a record of your assets, liabilities, and subsequent net worth at a particular time.

BENEFICIARY A person you designate in your will, insurance policy, or retirement plan to receive funds, assets, or proceeds when you die.

BLUE-CHIP STOCKS These are shares of well-known companies with solid financial histories and reputations of steady earnings and dividends.

BOND RATING This is the safety value of a particular bond as assigned by independent agencies, such as Standard & Poor's, that evaluate the possibility of default (that is, whether you will actually get the principal and interest when you are supposed to).

BONDS This is the debt of a corporation or the government. A bond buyer provides money to the institution, which in turn pays back the sum with interest at a specified time.

BROKERAGE An intermediary between buyers and sellers of stocks and other securities. There are three basic levels of brokerages. *Low-commission discount brokers* offer little or no advice, but are an inexpensive way to go. *Full-service brokers* help you make decisions and provide research materials and plenty of hand-holding, but you pay for it. *Online* brokers are the bargain basement and simply let you execute a trade over your computer without even talking to a person,

CAPITAL GAIN OR LOSS This is the amount you make or lose from selling one of your assets, such as your home.

CASH-VALUE LIFE INSURANCE A combination life insurance policy and savings plan. There are several types, including whole life, universal life, and variable life.

CERTIFICATE OF DEPOSIT (CD) This is an insured bank deposit with a guaranteed interest rate that is held for a set time period, usually three months, six months, one year, or five years.

CERTIFIED FINANCIAL PLANNER (CFP) The designation for financial planners who are certified by the CFP Board of Standards. A CFP must complete a series of courses and continuing education credits on an annual basis. These planners are fiduciaries and must make investment recommendations in your best interest.

CHARTERED FINANCIAL CONSULTANT (CHFC) Designation awarded to qualified financial planners by the American College of Financial Services in Bryn Mawr, Pennsylvania.

CHARTERED LIFE UNDERWRITER (CLU) This is a designation given to qualified life insurance agents by the American College of Financial Services.

CHILD SUPPORT Monthly payments, required by state law, that a noncustodial parent must provide to support his or her children. These are not taxable payments.

COBRA The Consolidated Omnibus Reconciliation Act is a federal law that requires your partner's company health plan to continue to offer you and any dependents coverage for at least 18 months if you have been divorced or separated or if your partner has died. You must pay the premiums. You have sixty days to decide to stay on your partner's plan.

COMMON-LAW PROPERTY Property divided according to who has title to the asset.

COMMON STOCK These are equity shares in any publicly traded company.

COMMUNITY PROPERTY Property and assets accumulated during your marriage are divided equally between the divorcing parties. Property acquired before the marriage or inherited is excluded. Community-property states are currently Arizona, California, Idaho, Louisiana, Nevada, New Mexico, Texas, Washington, and Wisconsin.

COMPOUNDING This is the combination of a principal investment and the subsequent interest it earns that keeps the pot growing month to month and year to year. The more the money compounds, the more interest an investment earns.

CREDIT REPORT This is your permanent record, so to speak, of your financial health as far as lenders are concerned. Every late payment, missed payment, and credit applied for is noted and recorded for at least seven years. A bad credit rating can make it hard for you to get a loan, land a job, or even open a bank account. Go to annualcreditreport.com for a checkup.

CYCLICAL STOCKS These are shares of companies whose earnings move up and down with the economy, such as carmakers and homebuilders.

DEDUCTIBLE This is the amount you will pay under an insurance plan before the insurer picks up the tab.

DEFINED BENEFIT PLAN This is a traditional pension plan in which an employer uses a formula based on salary and years of employment with the firm to devise an income to be paid to the employee or beneficiary on a regular basis at retirement.

DISABILITY INSURANCE This is insurance coverage that pays benefits if you are unable to work for a period of time due to physical or emotional problems.

DIVERSIFICATION Spreading your investment risk across many types of investments to mitigate risk.

DIVIDENDS Payouts to shareholders by a corporation based on a percentage of its earnings (may be in the form of cash or additional shares).

DOLLAR COST AVERAGING A method whereby you invest a fixed amount of money at preset intervals, regardless of price per share.

DOW JONES AVERAGES The Dow Industrial, Composite, Transportation, and Utility averages are indicators of how the stock market is faring. The Industrial consists of 30 major stocks, such as Disney and IBM. There are 20 stocks in the Transportation average and 15 stocks in the Utility average. The Composite consists of sixty-five stocks that are a combination of the others.

DURABLE POWER OF ATTORNEY Legal document by which you empower someone to handle your financial affairs if you are incapacitated but still alive.

EQUITABLE DISTRIBUTION This is the basic method of distributing property in forty states plus the District of Columbia. A court decides how to divide the assets of your marriage based on criteria such as need, earnings potential, and financial contribution to the marriage.

ESTATE PLAN This is your blueprint for the orderly disposition of your assets when you die. This should include writing a will, naming a guardian for your children, and designating an executor to handle your affairs. It should also address tax planning to minimize the tax burden levied on your estate.

ESTATE TAXES These are the taxes levied by federal and state governments on a deceased person's assets.

EXECUTOR This is the individual named in a will to handle the settlement of the estate.

401(K) PLAN This is a company's retirement benefit plan that allows employees to make regular, tax-deferred contributions from their salaries each pay period. Companies may match a portion of the employees' contributions.

403(B) PLAN Similar to a 401(k), these plans are offered to public employees and people who work for nonprofit organizations.

GROWTH MUTUAL FUNDS Mutual funds that invest in company stocks that are likely to appreciate over time. Capital gains is their objective.

GUARDIAN This is the person you select to take care of your children if they are under age eighteen when you die.

HEALTH-CARE PROXY A legal document in which you designate a person to make medical decisions for you if you are unable to do so. It can be paired with a living will.

INCOME FUNDS Mutual funds that invest their assets mostly in corporations (such as utilities) that pay dividends.

INDEX FUNDS Mutual funds that attempt to replicate a certain established stock index, like the S&P 500.

INDIVIDUAL RETIREMENT ACCOUNT (IRA) A tax-deferred pension plan that allows you to invest up to $2,000 annually, $4,000 if married filing jointly, in an account that is tax-free until you withdraw the money at retirement. There is a penalty for removing the funds before age 59½ and you must start withdrawing the money by age 70½.

INTERNATIONAL FUNDS These are mutual funds that invest in stocks of non-U.S. firms. Some invest in only one country or in a specific region.

INVESTMENT CLUB A group of people who research stock investments and pool their money together to invest regularly as one entity.

KEOGH PLAN This is a type of tax-deferred retirement plan for small-business owners or self-employed people. Up to 25 percent of income can be put into such a plan,

LIABILITY This is what you owe.

LIQUIDITY This is the measure of how fast you can get your money back from an investment. Treasuries and money markets are considered to be highly liquid. Real estate, on the other hand, is not.

LIVING TRUST This is a revocable trust that you establish while you are still living to make sure your assets are managed properly if you are disabled and unable to do so yourself.

LIVING WILL A legal document that spells out just how much medical intervention you desire if you have a terminal illness.

LOAD FUNDS These are mutual funds that levy an up-front sales charge, or commission, when you buy or sell. Most load funds are sold by full-service brokers.

MATURITY This is the date at which a bond must be paid in full.

MEDIATION A divorce process in which you and your soon-to-be ex hire a professional divorce mediator to work out your agreement. A lawyer will have to finalize the deal.

MONEY MARKET A federally insured bank account that typically pays higher interest than a regular savings account and requires a minimum investment.

MONEY MARKET FUND A mutual fund that invests only in short-term securities and is highly liquid.

MUNICIPAL BONDS Bonds issued by a local or state government and sold in denominations of $1,000 and $5,000. The interest from these bonds is free of federal and (usually) local and state taxes.

MUTUAL FUNDS A selection of stocks and bonds, or a mixture of investments, that are pooled together, sold as shares to individual investors, and managed by a professional money manager.

NATIONAL ASSOCIATION OF SECURITIES DEALERS (NASD) A membership association of brokerage firms and stock underwriters in the United States. They adhere to ethics guidelines, strict industry procedures, and disciplinary actions for rules violations.

NET ASSET VALUE The market value of a mutual fund share. The value is the total of all the fund's shares minus any liabilities divided by the number of outstanding shares.

NET WORTH Your assets minus your liabilities.

NO-LOAD FUNDS Mutual funds that do not charge sales commissions when you buy or sell.

PERSONAL FINANCIAL SPECIALIST This is the financial planning designation given to accountants approved by the American Institute of Certified Financial Accountants, which is headquartered in New York.

PRENUPTIAL AGREEMENT A legally binding agreement signed before marriage that spells out how your assets and your partner's will be divided in the event of death or divorce.

PRICE-TO-BOOK RATIO (P/B Ratio) is a ratio used to compare a stock's market value to its book value. It's computed by dividing the current closing price of the stock by the latest quarter's book value per share. The book value is a company's assets minus its liabilities.

PRICE-TO-EARNINGS RATIO (P/E ratio) is the ratio for valuing a corporation that measures its current share price in relation to its per-share earnings. The price-earnings ratio is also occasionally identified as the price multiple or the earnings multiple.

QUALIFIED DOMESTIC RELATIONS ORDER This is the state domestic relations court order requiring that an employee's retirement plan must be divided among an employee, a partner, and any children if there is a divorce.

RATE OF RETURN This is how much your invested money is likely to make in a given period of time.

RISK This is a measure of possible loss in value. Generally speaking, the riskier the investment, the higher return it is likely to have.

SECTOR FUNDS Mutual funds that buy stocks in just one industry, such as autos or biotechnology.

SECURITIES AND EXCHANGE COMMISSION (SEC) The SEC is the federal agency assigned to regulate the securities industry and protect investors from fraudulent activities.

SEP-IRA A retirement plan for the self-employed, known as the Simplified Employee Pension (or SEP) plan, in which an IRA is opened and up to 13 percent of net earnings can be contributed tax-deferred until retirement.

SOCIALLY CONSCIOUS FUNDS Mutual funds that buy shares only in firms that do not conflict with certain social priorities. For example, they might avoid companies that sell tobacco-related products or choose companies with excellent environmental records.

SOCIAL SECURITY These are the retirement funds paid by the federal government, provided you have been employed for at least forty quarters.

STOCKS These are shares in a company that are sold to raise capital. There are more than eight thousand publicly traded companies.

TERM LIFE INSURANCE This is straight life insurance with no extra cash value. You receive the benefit when your partner dies.

TREASURY BILL This is a short-term debt instrument issued by the federal government. The bills mature in periods of three months, six months, or one year. Your minimum purchase is $10,000.

TREASURY BOND This is a long-term debt instrument, issued by the federal government, that matures in ten to thirty years. The bonds sell in denominations of $1,000 and pay interest twice a year.

TREASURY NOTE This is a medium-term debt instrument, issued by the federal government, that matures in one to ten years. The minimum purchase is $5,000 for under four years; over four years, it's $1,000. Interest is paid twice a year.

UNIVERSAL LIFE INSURANCE This is a type of insurance in which part of the premium goes toward buying insurance and the remainder is invested.

U.S. SAVINGS BONDS Series EE bonds are issued by the federal government. You can purchase them through most banks, credit unions, and S&Ls. All interest is free of state and local taxes.

VESTING When employers offer 401(k) accounts to employees, they typically match a percentage of the employees' contributions. But those employer-provided funds are not awarded to the employee for a fixed number of years of employment, usually five, which is the vesting period.

WILL A legal document stating how you want your assets to be dispersed following your death and naming a guardian for minor children.

ZERO-COUPON BOND A bond that sells at a steep discount from its face value and pays no interest until it matures, at which time you can redeem it at the full face value.

ABOUT THE AUTHOR

Elizabeth Dranitzke, Photopia

Kerry Hannon is a nationally recognized expert and strategist on career transitions, personal finance, and retirement, especially for older women. She is a frequent TV and radio commentator and is a sought-after keynote speaker at conferences across the country. Kerry focuses on empowering yourself to do more with your career and personal finances—now and for the future.

She has spent more than two decades covering all aspects of careers, business and personal finance as a columnist, editor, and writer for the nation's leading media companies, including *The New York Times, Forbes, Money, U.S. News & World Report, USA Today,* and *The Wall Street Journal.* She has appeared as a career and financial expert on *The Dr. Phil Show* ABC, CBS, CNBC, NBC *Nightly News*, NPR, and PBS.

Kerry is currently a columnist and regular contributor to *The New York Times*, a contributing writer for *Money* magazine, AARP's Work and Jobs Expert and Great Jobs columnist, contributing editor and Second Verse columnist at *Forbes,* and the PBS website NextAvenue.org expert and columnist on personal finance, wealth management and careers for boomer women.

Kerry is the award-winning author of a dozen books, including national bestseller *Great Jobs for Everyone 50 +: Finding Work that Keeps You Happy. Healthy... and Pays the Bills, Getting the Job You Want After 50 For Dummies*; *Love Your Job: The New Rules for Career Happiness* and *What's Next? Finding Your Passion and Your Dream Job in Your Forties, Fifties and Beyond.*

Follow Kerry on Twitter @KerryHannon, visit her website at KerryHannon.com, and check out her LinkedIn profile at linkedin.com/in/kerryhannon.

Advance Praise for *Money Confidence*

"For any woman who finds herself newly single after a long-term marriage or relationship, Kerry Hannon offers an invaluable guide to getting back on your feet financially—critical knowledge, at a time when the last thing on your mind may be money. Kerry's clear, smart advice reflects her deep knowledge of the subject and, just as importantly, her tremendous compassion for what readers are going through."

–Diane Harris, former editor-in-chief, *Money*

"Money Confidence: Really Smart Moves for Newly Single Women is a must-read for women entering a new stage in life as they maneuver a changing financial reality. The book provides practical strategies for a wide range of difficult decisions they will need to make to ensure their future economic security."

–M. Cindy Hounsell, President, Women's Institute for a Secure Retirement

"Money Confidence could be the best investment a newly single widow or divorcee can make. The book is laden with practical, timely advice on everything from investing mojo to budgeting for your new life, and Hannon's decade-by-decade Money-Savvy Checklist alone is worth the purchase price."

–Richard Eisenberg, Money & Security channel editor, Nextavenue.org

"Kerry Hannon is the go-to source to help women find financial security and confidence. *Money Confidence: Really*

Smart Financial Moves for Newly Single Women provides divorced or widowed women with a fundamental tool-kit that will change their lives. Hannon skillfully embraces the need for women, who find themselves on their own, to take control of their financial future, take responsibility, and continue to educate themselves about financial choices. Importantly, read this book to find out how to take a look at your financial situation, make decisions based on your individual needs, and make sure you understand an investment before you put your money into it."

–Don Blandin, president and CEO
of the Investor Protection Trust (IPT) and
the Investor Protection Institute (IPI)

Money Confidence is an essential go-to guide for women who find themselves alone after a divorce or death of a spouse. With inspiring stories about women who have successfully navigated through the most difficult of financial situations, Kerry Hannon shares expert insights in a simple step-by-step guide. In doing so, she lovingly offers an empowering message for newly single women that they can take control of their finances as they move forward their lives."

–Catherine Collinson, nationally recognized
retirement expert, thought leader,
researcher, and advocate